Editor
Mara Ellen Guckian

Editor in Chief
Brent L. Fox, M. Ed.

Creative Director
Sarah M. Fournier

Cover Artist
Sarah Kim

Illustrator
Mark Mason

Art Coordinator
Renée Mc Elwee

Imaging
Amanda R. Harter

Publisher
Mary D. Smith, M.S. Ed.

For standards correlations, please visit
*http://www.teachercreated.com
/standards/*.

LET'S GET THE DAY STARTED
Science

TCR 8266

- Start the day off right with engaging, standards-based science passages and writing activities.

- Each unit includes non-fiction passages, vocabulary activities, and supplemental worksheets. All content is designed to encourage students to "show what they know."

- Unit activities help students improve comprehension skills from recall to critical thinking.

- Photographs or illustrations are provided to boost student understanding of important science concepts.

Teacher Created Resources

Author
Tracy Edmunds, M.A. Ed.

Teacher Created Resources
12621 Western Avenue
Garden Grove, CA 92841
www.teachercreated.com

ISBN: 978-1-4206-8266-3

©2020 Teacher Created Resources
Reprinted, 2020
Made in U.S.A.

Teacher Created Resources

Table of Contents

Table of Contents *(cont.)*

Introduction

Science is the study of the world around us. Students experience science every day without knowing it! Learning about how the world works can be fascinating, but sometimes, students are intimidated or confused by complex science concepts. This book seeks to break down big ideas such as waves, energy, and plate tectonics, making them more accessible for sixth-grade students. The passages in this book contain high-interest topics that are aligned with NGSS standards for the grade level. From exploring the senses in animals and humans to discovering invisible forces, students will enjoy practicing their informational reading skills with interesting science topics.

This book is divided into three sections:

Physical Science

Life Science

Earth and Space Science

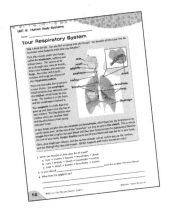

Within each section are a number of units, each of which explores important science topics. Each unit has 4–9 pages and features reading passages, response questions, and science-related activity sheets. Within each science discipline, the units are sequential and build upon one another, and passages are sequential within a unit.

Some units incorporate photographs into student activities. These add a realistic element to the writing prompts and engage students by providing a real-life connection for their learning. When making photocopies of these pages, it is best to use the photo setting so the images are easier to see. You may also choose to supplement certain passages with related photographs or other visual aids you might have available.

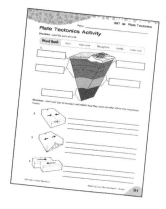

Teachers should not feel restricted by a daily warm-up activity. Sometimes, schedules change. A morning assembly, a make-up lesson, or just an extra-busy day can easily throw off the classroom schedule for days. A teacher never knows what his or her week is going to look like. *Let's Get This Day Started: Science* units do not need to be completed every day or even every other day. Teachers can take their time and arrange the activities to fit their own schedules. A teacher may choose to do a unit a week (one passage a day) or spread a unit out over a few weeks. There is no right or wrong way.

These pages are meant to supplement, not substitute for, a science curriculum. Use them in conjunction with science lessons whenever possible.

How to Use This Book

When introducing each new science topic, a teacher may choose to have the class read the passages together as a group before asking them to read each passage on their own. A teacher may also choose to have students reread passages after a science lesson or unit to reinforce and review learning.

Another way to introduce a new science topic is to begin with the *Word Study* activity sheet included in each unit. A teacher may choose to review the science vocabulary as a group before reading the passages. This will allow students to become acquainted with some of the more difficult terms and be on the lookout for them when reading the passages.

The multiple-choice questions in *Let's Get This Day Started: Science* assess all levels of comprehension—from recall to critical thinking. These questions offer an opportunity to teach students test-taking skills. If an answer choice includes an unfamiliar word, the correct answer can still be found using the process of elimination. Remind students to read every answer choice! If the answer doesn't jump out at them, they can get it right by crossing out the wrong answers first.

The missing words or phrases for fill-in-the-blank questions can be found within the reading passage. These questions reinforce important scientific vocabulary and concepts.

Short, written-response questions require students to connect new learning and vocabulary to their own experiences or to apply the concepts in the passage to a new situation. These questions are intended to encourage students to "show what they know." Responses will vary based on students' reading, writing, and prior knowledge.

Use the *Tracking Sheet* (page 107) to keep track of which passages you have given to your students, or distribute copies of the sheet for students to monitor their own progress.

An answer key is provided in the back (pages 108–112). It is important to review how students have answered written-response questions. These answers will vary depending on a student's experiences and prior knowledge.

Name: _____

Natural Resources

Look around you and think about where the things you see come from. What is your chair or the clothes and shoes you are wearing made of? What is powering the lights in the room? And how are you getting the energy to read this?

Everything we have or use comes from **natural resources**—things that occur naturally on Earth that humans did not make. We use natural resources all the time. We breathe air. We drink water and use it to clean ourselves and our things. We also need water to grow crops. We eat plants and some animal products, such as meat, eggs, and milk. We use wood from trees to build things and to make paper. We use rocks and **minerals** to make metal products. We generate electricity and make gasoline for vehicles using **fossil fuels** from deep under the ground. Everything comes from natural resources!

Let's go back to the things you see around you. What natural resources are used to make them?

If your chair is made of wood, that wood comes from trees. If it is metal, it is made from minerals in rocks, and if it is plastic, it is made from fossil fuels. Some chairs are made of all three!

Your clothes may be made of cotton from a plant, leather from an animal, or **synthetic** fabrics made from fossil fuels. Synthetic fabrics are human-made to resemble natural fabrics.

The lights in the room are powered by electricity, which may have been generated by a power plant burning fossil fuels, by wind-blowing turbines, or even from solar collectors gathering power from the Sun.

You get your energy from the food you eat.

1. Which of these is not a *natural resource*?
   a. wood   b. water   c. laptop   d. soil

2. How do you use air and sunlight?

   _____

   _____

3. Write one thing you use that is made (or partially made) from each resource.

   trees _____

   minerals _____

   fossil fuels _____

   cotton _____

Name: _____

Word Study—Natural and Synthetic

Directions: Study the definitions. Then, use each vocabulary word in a sentence that relates to the information from this unit.

chemical reaction—occurs when molecules that make up a substance are broken apart and rearranged into different molecules

_____

_____

decompose—to break down into smaller parts; to decay

_____

_____

fossil fuels—the remains of ancient plants and animals buried underground for millions of years; oil, coal, and natural gas used to make fuels and synthetic materials

_____

_____

minerals—substances formed naturally in the ground that are used to make metals, fertilizers, sand, and other products

_____

_____

molecules—the smallest units of a substance that have all the properties of that substance; the building blocks that make everything around us

_____

_____

natural resources—things that occur naturally on Earth and that are not human-made

_____

physical properties—characteristics of matter that may be observed and measured (color, length, hardness, etc.)

_____

_____

synthetic—a product created when a natural resource is changed through a chemical reaction; something that is produced artificially, especially by chemical means

_____

_____

Name: _____

Using Natural Resources

We use some **natural resources** just as they are. We breathe air and get vitamin D, light, and warmth from sunlight. In some places, you can eat fruit right off a tree, but not many of us eat plants directly from nature.

Most natural resources must be changed in order for us to use them. The plants we eat are farmed, harvested, and prepared for eating. Other plants, like cotton, are turned into fabrics and other fiber products. Rocks and **minerals** must be mined from the ground and changed into metal products such as steel and iron. Water must be cleaned before we can use it. You wouldn't want to drink water directly from a stream or lake—it might have bacteria in it that can make you sick.

Wood is a natural resource that comes from trees. We cut down trees, saw the wood into lumber, and then use it to make buildings, furniture, flooring, and cabinets. Some wood is **pulped**, or torn into little bits, and then combined with water and chemicals and rolled out to make paper and cardboard.

Fossil fuels are the remains of ancient plants and animals that have been buried underground for millions of years. Pressure turns these remains into fossil fuels, such as oil and natural gas. We pump them up from deep under the ground and change them into gasoline and heating oil, plastics, medicines, paints, clothing, and more.

1. True or False? We use most natural resources just as they are found in nature.   **True   False**

2. *Fossil fuels* are _____.
   a. used to make gasoline   **c.** found deep underground
   b. used to make plastic   **d.** all of the above

3. What are some natural resources you have used today? Explain how you used them.

Resource	Use

Name: _____

Synthetic Materials—Plastic

Think about things around you that are made of plastic. Water bottles, plastic bags, sports equipment, and maybe even your chair can be made of plastic. Plastic is found in computers and cell phones, cars and airplanes, clothing and shoes, and toothbrushes and pens. There are more products made from plastic than any other material.

We know that everything comes from natural resources. So, what natural resource is used to make plastic? Most plastic is made from **fossil fuels**, which are the remains of ancient plants and animals. We have to dig very deep to get fossil fuels out of the ground where they have been buried for millions of years.

How do fossil fuels become plastic? They are heated and mixed with other things to cause a **chemical reaction**. In a chemical reaction, **molecules** are broken apart and rearranged. This means plastic is a **synthetic**, or human-made, material. Depending on the chemicals used, plastics can be hard or soft, stretchy or stiff, clear or cloudy.

One of the properties that makes plastic useful is that it lasts a long time. But this also makes plastic a problem. Natural materials, like paper and leftover food, will **decompose**, or break down, over time. Plastics will not! It can take from 400 to 1,000 years for plastic to decompose.

Think about it: If George Washington and the Founding Fathers had been drinking water from plastic bottles when they signed the Declaration of Independence, their bottles would still be around today.

1. What is a *chemical reaction*?
    a. It occurs when molecules break apart and are rearranged.
    b. It is a way to make natural resources.
    c. It is something that lasts a long time.

2. What are some things you use every day that are made of plastic?

    _____ _____ _____

3. What are some problems caused by plastics lasting a long time?

    _____

    _____

    _____

Name: _____

Natural vs. Synthetic

A school is trying to decide whether to use **natural** grass or **synthetic** (artificial) grass for its new sports field. There are advantages and disadvantages for each choice.

➡ The natural grass would grow from seeds planted in the soil. The natural grass will require water, fertilizer, mowing, and weeding on a regular basis.

➡ The synthetic grass will be more expensive to put in, but it is made of plastic and would be rolled out on the field. It can get hot and can hurt when you slide on it.

Natural

Synthetic

1. Fill in the chart below. Think about what it would be like to play on each surface, what it will take to care for each type of grass, and how long each kind of grass might last.

	Natural Grass	Synthetic Grass
Advantages		
Disadvantages		

2. Which choice would you make for your school? _____

   Why? _____

   _____

Name: _____

Physical and Chemical Changes

Have you ever watched an ice cube melt? Or wood burn? These are two examples of changes in matter.

Physical Changes

When an ice cube melts, the water changes from solid to liquid, but it is still water. This is an example of a **physical change**. The **states of matter** change, but the **molecules** that make up the matter stay the same. The state of water can change into liquid, solid, or gas (water vapor), and the molecules are still H_2O.

Physical change may cause a **substance**, a particular kind of matter, to change shapes or states, but the molecules stay the same and no new substances are produced.

More examples of physical changes:

- boiling water changing to water vapor
- crushing an aluminum can
- mixing sand with water
- breaking glass
- chopping wood

Chemical Changes

When wood burns, a **chemical change** takes place. The **molecules** of the wood change—the bonds that hold them together are broken, and new ones are formed. The molecules in the wood change into ash and smoke, and energy is released in the form of light and heat.

Chemical change always produces a new **substance**, but a physical change does not.

More examples of chemical changes:

- cooking an egg
- rusting iron
- rotting food
- exploding fireworks

1. In a _____ change, the molecules of matter change.

   a. physical   **b.** chemical

2. *Chemical change* always produces a new _____.

3. What is the main difference between a *chemical change* and a *physical change*?

   _____

   _____

Name: _____

Word Study—Physical and Chemical Change

Directions: Write each term in the Word Bank before its definition. Then, add an example or two using words or pictures.

Word Bank	chemical change irreversible molecule properties substance evidence matter physical change state of matter

	Term	Definition	Examples
1		anything that has mass and takes up space; everything around you	
2		matter that has specific properties and is made up of specific molecules	
3		things that can be measured or observed about matter (color, hardness, weight, etc.)	
4		one of the forms in which matter can exist	
5		the smallest unit of a chemical compound that can take part in a chemical reaction	
6		a change in matter that alters the properties of a substance but does not change its molecules	
7		a change in matter that rearranges molecules and creates a new substance	
8		a change that cannot be undone	
9		anything that shows that something is true or has really happened	

Name: _____

Evidence of Chemical Change

Have you ever used a glow stick? When you bend the glow stick and hear a pop, you are breaking a small container inside the stick. This causes two **substances** in the stick to mix together, which makes the glow that you see. That glow is **evidence**, proof, that a **chemical change** has taken place.

During a chemical change, the **molecules** of a substance are broken apart, joined together, or both. This makes a new substance with new and different **properties**. Nothing is ever destroyed or created in a chemical change. The same particles that made up the molecules before the change still exist after the change. The particles are just rearranged into different combinations to make different substances.

How can you tell whether a chemical or a physical change has taken place? It's not always easy to tell if a new substance has formed. Look at the table on the right for types of **evidence** that a chemical change has taken place.

Warning! A change in texture or hardness does not always mean a chemical change has taken place. Some physical changes also cause **matter** to change texture or hardness, such as water changing to ice.

Changes	Examples	
color	toast turning brown	
smell	smelly, rotten food	
gas	mixing vinegar and baking soda creates a lot of bubbles	
light	glow sticks	
heat	burning candle	
change in texture or hardness	cooking an egg	

1. What is *evidence*?
   - **a.** anything that shows that something happened or is true
   - **b.** when two substances mix together to make a new substance
   - **c.** when molecules are rearranged to create a chemical change

2. _____ is created or destroyed in a chemical change.

3. How can you tell if a chemical change has happened? _____

_____

Baking soda and vingar reaction, Kate Ter Harr (*www.flickr.com/photos/katerha/*), CC BY 2.0.

Name: _____

Reversible and Irreversible Changes

Humpty Dumpty will be the first one to tell you: Some changes are irreversible. Once you crack an egg, not even all the king's men can put it back together again.

An **irreversible change**, such as cracking and cooking an egg, changes the egg permanently. It cannot be uncracked or uncooked.

➡ Once wood has burned and turned to ash, it can't be changed back into wood. The change is irreversible.

A **reversible change** is when a substance changes, but it can be changed back.

➡ Water can freeze into ice and then melt back into water again.

Physical changes can be either reversible or irreversible.

➡ Blowing up a balloon without tying it is a reversible, physical change. The balloon changes shape when you blow it up. When you let the air out, it goes back to its original shape.

➡ Grinding wood into sawdust is an irreversible physical change. You can't change the sawdust back into a piece of wood.

Chemical changes are usually irreversible. In a chemical change, a new substance is created. It is very difficult or impossible to change the new substance back into what you had before.

➡ Once you bake cookies, you can't turn them back into dough.

Note: Some chemical changes *can* be reversed, but only by other chemical changes. For example, the copper in a penny can react with oxygen in the air, creating a new substance called copper oxide. This makes the penny look dark. You can reverse this change by putting the penny in vinegar. The vinegar reacts with the copper oxide and changes back to copper and oxygen, making the penny copper-colored again.

Directions: For each change listed below, circle *physical* or *chemical*, then *reversible* or *irreversible*.

1	stretching a rubber band	physical chemical	reversible irreversible
2	grinding wood into sawdust	physical chemical	reversible irreversible
3	folding paper	physical chemical	reversible irreversible
4	lighting a match	physical chemical	reversible irreversible
5	melting chocolate	physical chemical	reversible irreversible
6	mowing grass	physical chemical	reversible irreversible
7	turning milk into cheese	physical chemical	reversible irreversible

Name: _____

Which Kind of Change?

Directions: For each example of a change in matter, circle either *chemical* or *physical* and either *reversible* or *irreversible*. Explain how you know what kind of change it is.

1	chemical physical
	_____ _____ _____
	reversible irreversible

2	chemical physical
	_____ _____ _____
	reversible irreversible

3	chemical physical
	_____ _____ _____
	reversible irreversible

4	chemical physical
	_____ _____ _____
	reversible irreversible

Directions: Draw and explain your own example of a change in matter.

5	chemical physical
	_____ _____ _____
	reversible irreversible

Name: _____

Non-Contact Forces

What happens when you kick a ball? Your foot puts **force** on the ball, making the ball move. This is called a **contact force** because your foot makes contact with, or touches, the ball.

What happens when you jump up into the air? You fall back down to the ground. You can't see anything pushing you down—there is no contact force. So what force makes you come back down? A **non-contact force**!

Non-contact forces push or pull on objects without touching them. There are many kinds of contact forces, but there are not very many non-contact forces. Here are two types of non-contact forces:

Gravitational Force

When you jump up, **gravitational force** is the force that brings you back down to the ground. Gravitational force, or as we call it, **gravity,** is an invisible force that pulls objects together. We feel Earth's gravitational force pulling down on us and on everything around us all the time.

Electromagnetic Force

Electromagnetic force is all around us—and in us! It's what holds **atoms** together. Atoms are what everything is made of, so electromagnetic force holds everything together! We can see electromagnetic force working in electricity and magnets. Depending on what the atoms are doing, this electromagnetic force can **repel** (push) or **attract** (pull). It can make your hair stand up, it can make a magnet work, or it can store information in a computer. Electromagnetic forces can even cause lightning!

1. A *non-contact* force can _____.
   - **a.** pull on things
   - **b.** push things
   - **c.** act on objects without touching them
   - **d.** all of the above

2. _____ forces pull objects together.

3. _____ forces can push or pull.

4. How is a *contact force* different from a *non-contact force*?

   _____

   _____

   _____

Name: _____

Word Study—Non-Contact Forces

Directions: Read the definitions in the graphic organizer. Use the Word Bank to find the correct word or phrase to match each definition. ***Note:*** One word will be used twice.

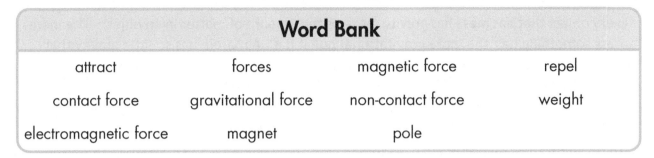

Word Bank			
attract	forces	magnetic force	repel
contact force	gravitational force	non-contact force	weight
electromagnetic force	magnet	pole	

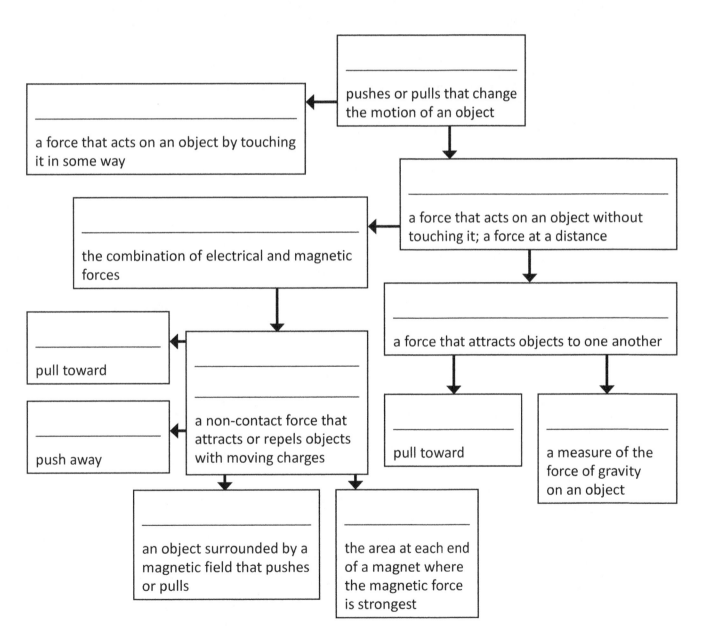

_____
pushes or pulls that change the motion of an object

_____
a force that acts on an object by touching it in some way

_____
a force that acts on an object without touching it; a force at a distance

_____
the combination of electrical and magnetic forces

_____
a force that attracts objects to one another

_____
pull toward

_____
a non-contact force that attracts or repels objects with moving charges

_____
push away

_____
pull toward

_____
a measure of the force of gravity on an object

_____
an object surrounded by a magnetic field that pushes or pulls

_____
the area at each end of a magnet where the magnetic force is strongest

Name: _____

Gravity

Gravity is an invisible force that pulls objects together. It is a **non-contact force**, which means it can pull objects without actually touching them.

Every object that has **mass** has gravity. Mass is the amount of matter in an object. The more mass something has, the more **gravitational pull** it has. A marble has so little gravity that it's very difficult to measure it. You have gravity, but it's very weak because you are not very big. Earth's gravitational pull is strong because it has so much mass. Different planets in our solar system have different gravitational strengths depending on their masses. The gravity of the Sun and the planets pulling on one another are what keeps our solar system together.

We experience gravity all the time as it pulls us toward the center of Earth. It causes things to fall, and to speed up as they get closer to the ground. Gravity also gives things **weight**. Weight is a measure of how strongly gravity is pulling on something. That's why astronauts weigh less on the Moon—its gravitational pull is weaker than Earth's because it has less mass.

The closer two things are to each other, the stronger the gravitational pull between them will be. That's why we need rockets to send an object into space. It takes a lot of power to overcome the pull of Earth's gravity when a rocket is close to the surface. The farther away it gets, the weaker the gravitational pull becomes.

1. *Gravity _____.*
   - **a.** gives things weight
   - **b.** is a contact force
   - **c.** is the same for all objects
   - **d.** is a visible force

2. The more _____ something has, the stronger its gravity.

3. Give three examples of how we experience the *gravitational pull* of Earth.

   Example 1 _____

   Example 2 _____

   Example 3 _____

4. Number these objects in order of their gravitational pull, from *least* to *most*.

marble	human	Earth	mountain	elephant	Moon	Sun
☐	☐	☐	☐	☐	☐	☐

#8266 *Let's Get This Day Started: Science*

Name: _____

Magnetic Force

Have you ever played with a **magnet**? It's almost like magic, isn't it? You can hold a magnet near some paper clips and watch them move, seemingly all by themselves. It isn't magic—it's science! **Magnetic force** is a **non-contact force**, which means it affects things without touching them.

Magnets have two ends called **poles**—a north pole and a south pole. Sound familiar? Yes, Earth has a north pole and a south pole, too! Earth is like a giant magnet!

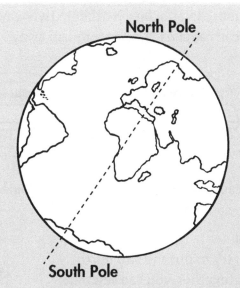

North Pole

South Pole

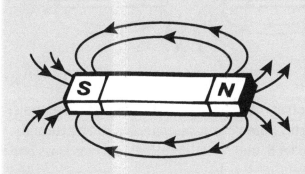

Magnetic lines of force are imaginary lines that help us understand how magnets work. They show the **magnetic field**, which is the area around a magnet where its magnetic force can affect objects. The lines go through the magnet from the south pole to the north pole. When they go out of the magnet at the north pole, they curve around and go back to the south pole.

Note: A magnetic field does not have the same strength all around a magnet. The magnetic force is strongest at the poles and weaker in the middle of the magnet. Also, magnetic force is strongest near a magnet. The farther away you get, the weaker the force becomes.

1. The area around a magnet in which there is *magnetic force* is called its _____.
   a. magnetic lines   **b.** magnetic pole   **c.** magnetic field

2. Magnetic lines of force go through a magnet from the _____ pole

   to the _____ pole.

3. Magnetic force is strongest at the

   _____

   of a magnet.

4. Draw the magnetic lines of force for the magnet in this box. Include arrows to show direction going from **S** to **N**. ⟶

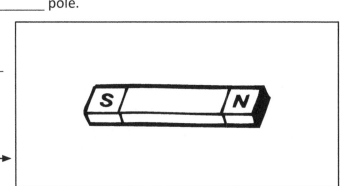

Name: _____

Attract or Repel?

Magnets can affect each other in two ways. They can **attract** each other, or pull closer, or they can **repel** each other, or push away.

Attract

When you hold the north pole of one magnet and the south pole of another magnet near each other, the opposite poles will be attracted to each other. They will pull toward each other. This is because the magnetic lines of force line up from one magnet to the other and keep going in the same direction.

Repel

If you try to put the two north poles together, you can see that the magnetic lines of force move in opposite directions. They push against each other. The "like" poles will **repel**, or push away, from each other.

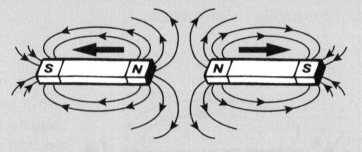

Magnets attract some metals, such as iron and cobalt. We call these **ferromagnetic** materials. Ferromagnetic materials are attracted by magnets. Some of these materials can be turned into magnets! Some metals, such as copper and lead, and other materials, such as glass and plastic, are not affected by magnetic force.

1. What will happen if you try to put the south poles of two magnets together? Why?

   _____

   _____

   _____

2. What will happen if you try to put the north pole of one magnet near the south pole of a second magnet? Why?

   _____

   _____

   _____

3. What do we call metals that are attracted by magnetic force?

   _____

Name: _____

What Is a Wave?

When you hear the word *wave*, what do you think about? Many of us think of an ocean wave crashing onto a beach, but that's only one kind of wave. There are waves all around us—sound waves, light waves, radio waves, microwaves, and more.

What is a **wave**? Waves are a way that energy moves from place to place. A wave always starts with energy.

➡ Waves in the ocean are started by the energy of the wind.

➡ Your voice is sound waves started by the energy of vibrations in your vocal cords.

➡ The energy of an earthquake can start seismic waves that move through the ground.

Some waves travel through **matter**. The matter that a wave's energy travels through is called its **medium**. Waves in the ocean travel through the medium of water. When you talk to a friend, the sound waves travel through the medium of air. The matter in a medium does not move along with the wave. The small bits, or **particles**, of the medium are moved up and down or back and forth by the wave's energy and end up back where they started.

Have you ever seen a crowd do "The Wave" in a sports stadium? Think about how that wave works. Does each person move all the way around the stadium? No! The people only move up and down at their seats. The energy moves around the stadium.

Energy travels forward in a wave, but the matter of the medium always returns to its starting point. Imagine a boat in the middle of a lake. As a small wave moves beneath it, how does the boat move?

The boat moves up and then down again and ends up back where it started. It doesn't travel along with the wave. The water underneath the boat is doing the same thing. It moves up and down as the wave passes through. If water traveled along with waves, all the water in the lake would eventually end up on the shore!

1. A *wave* always starts with _____.
   a. wind   **b.** energy   **c.** sound

2. The *matter* that a wave travels through is its _____.

3. What is a *wave*? _____

_____

Name: _____

Word Study—Mechanical Waves—Part 1

Directions: Read the definition for each word. Then, use the word in a sentence to help you remember its meaning.

Word	Definition	Sentence
matter	anything that has mass and takes up space; everything around you	_____ _____ _____
mechanical waves	waves that can only travel through a medium	_____ _____ _____
medium	matter that a wave travels through	_____ _____ _____
particles	small bits of matter	_____ _____ _____
waves	a way that energy moves from place to place	_____ _____ _____

Directions: Fill in each blank with one of the terms.

1. In a wave, the _____ of matter move a little bit and end up back where they started.

2. Ocean waves travel through the _____ of water.

3. Sound waves are _____, so they can travel through air, but not through empty space.

4. Light energy travels in _____ through the universe.

5. The air you breathe, the water you drink, and your body are all made of

_____.

Name: _____

Word Study—Mechanical Waves—Part 2

Directions: For each word, read the definition and draw a sketch or diagram to help you remember its meaning.

Word	Definition	Sketch or Diagram
transverse wave	a wave in which the particles move perpendicular to the direction of the wave	
longitudinal wave	a wave in which the particles move parallel to the direction of the wave	
parallel	side by side; going in the same direction	
perpendicular	at a right angle to	

Directions: Fill in each blank with one of the terms. Then, answer the question.

1. In a _____ , the particles move parallel to the direction of the wave.

2. In a _____ , the particles move perpendicular to the direction of the wave.

3. _____ lines are at right angles to each other.

4. _____ lines go in the same direction and never meet.

5. What kind of wave is shown below?   **transverse wave**   **longitudinal wave**

   How do you know? _____

Name: _____

Mechanical Waves

Try this: Press your ear to your desk and tap gently on the desk. Can you hear the sound through the desk? The sound energy is carried by **mechanical waves** traveling through the solid matter of the desk.

Mechanical waves can only travel through a **medium**, or some sort of matter. They cannot travel through empty space. The energy in a mechanical wave travels when the particles in matter bump into one another. One particle passes energy to the next, which passes it to the next, and so on. It is similar to dominoes falling in a line. Each domino bumps into the next. The energy is transferred along the line.

The particles in a mechanical wave don't always move side to side like dominoes. Particles can move in different ways depending on the kind of mechanical wave it is and the medium. They can move up and down, side to side, or in circles. Particles can move closer together (contract) and farther apart (expand).

Remember, in a wave, the particles of matter move a little bit and end up back where they started. It's the *energy* that moves from place to place.

Mechanical waves include waves on the surface of water, sound waves, and seismic waves that travel along the ground in an earthquake. Mechanical waves can travel through gases, liquids, or solids, such as when you heard sound waves traveling through your desk.

1. In a *wave*, the _____ moves along from one place to another.

   a. energy   **b.** matter   **c.** medium

2. *Mechanical waves* can only travel through _____.

3. Name the three states of matter that mechanical waves can travel through.

   _____   _____   _____

Name: _____

Transverse Waves

All waves are either transverse waves or longitudinal waves, depending on how the particles move.

In a **transverse wave**, the particles move **perpendicular** to the direction of the wave. Ocean waves are transverse waves—the water molecules move up and down as the wave moves across the surface of the ocean.

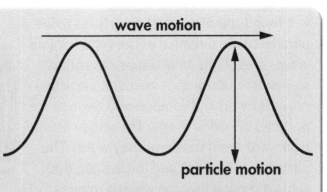

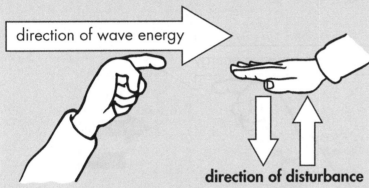

Try this: Point sideways with one hand. Hold your other hand out flat (to the side) and move it up and down. This is a simple model of the movement in a transverse wave. Your pointing hand shows the direction of the wave energy, and your other hand demonstrates the movement of the particles.

Here is another way to think about a transverse wave. Imagine you have a rope or a string. You tie one end to something that doesn't move. You grab the other end with your hand and move the rope up and down. The energy you put into the rope moves away from you along the rope. The rope itself moves up and down. This is a transverse wave.

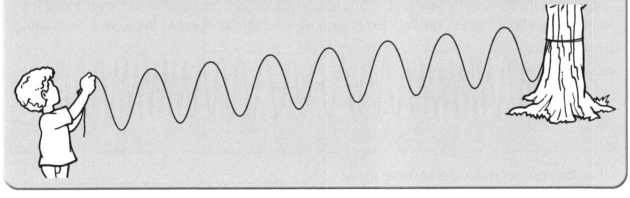

1. In a *transverse wave*, the particles move _____ to the direction of the wave.

2. What would happen if you laid a rope on the floor and moved it side to side?

   _____

3. What kind of wave would travel along the rope? _____

   How do you know? _____

   _____

Name: _____

Longitudinal Waves

In a **longitudinal wave**, the particles move **parallel** to the direction of the wave. Sound waves are longitudinal waves. As sound waves move through a medium, particles move forward and compress up close to the particles ahead of them. Then, they move backward again to where they were. The particles move back and forth along the same direction that the wave is moving.

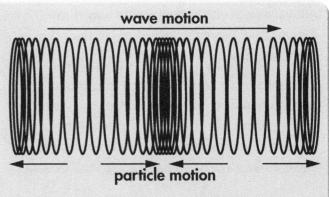

Try this: Point sideways with one hand. Hold your other hand up in front of you, and move it back and forth to the left and right. This is a simple model of the movement in a longitudinal wave. Your pointing hand shows the direction of the wave energy, and your other hand demonstrates the movement of the particles.

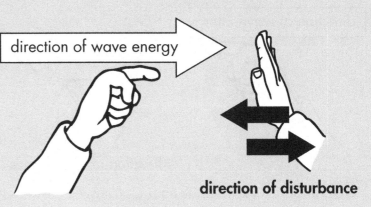

Here is another way to think about a longitudinal wave. Imagine you have a Slinky® toy. You lay the toy on a table and have a friend hold one end very still. You pull back on your end and then push forward quickly (without letting go). The energy from your hand moves along the Slinky toward your friend. The coils press together and spread apart as the wave moves along.

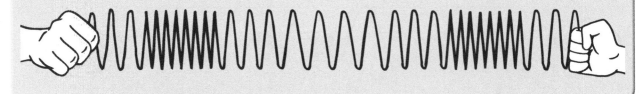

1. In a *longitudinal wave*, the particles move _____

   to the direction of the wave.

2. What would happen if you held one end of the Slinky and moved it up and down?

   _____

   _____

3. What kind of wave would that create? _____

   How do you know? _____

   _____

Name: _____

Electromagnetic Waves

Energy travels through space from the Sun to Earth in **waves**. Without this energy from the Sun, life could not exist on Earth.

We know that in empty space there is no air or other **medium** for the waves to travel through. So how does the Sun's energy get here? The Sun's energy does not travel in mechanical waves. It travels in **electromagnetic waves**. Electromagnetic waves occur when an electric field and a magnetic field move together.

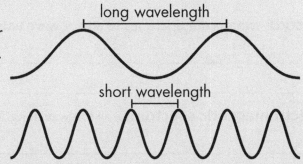

Electromagnetic waves are light waves, but not just the visible light we see. There are many types of electromagnetic waves we can't see. These waves can travel through matter or through empty space. These waves do not need matter to transfer energy.

Each type of light has a different **wavelength**. A wavelength is a measure of how spread out a wave is.

➡ Waves with a *long* wavelength are stretched far apart.

➡ Waves with a *short* wavelength are squeezed together.

Scientists organize electromagnetic waves in order of wavelength. This is called the **electromagnetic spectrum**. **Visible light**, which we can see, is in the middle of the spectrum. At one end, gamma rays and X-rays have very short wavelengths and a lot of energy. At the other end, radio waves and microwaves have very long wavelengths and less energy.

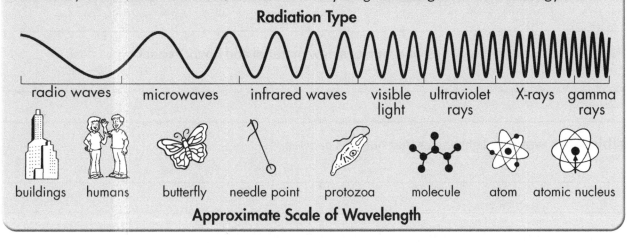

1. The *electromagnetic spectrum* organizes waves in order of _____.
   a. wavelength   b. energy   c. visibility

2. *Electromagnetic waves* can travel through both _____ and

   _____ _____.

3. What do we call the kind of electromagnetic waves can we see?

   _____

Name: _____

Word Study—Electromagnetic Waves

Directions: Study the definitions. Then, use each vocabulary word in a sentence that relates to the information from this unit.

absorb—what a material does to accept wave energy

_____

_____

electromagnetic spectrum—all the wavelengths of light organized from longest to shortest

_____

_____

electromagnetic wave—a wave that does not need a medium to transfer energy

_____

_____

matter—anything that has mass and takes up space; everything around you

_____

_____

medium—matter that a wave travels through

_____

_____

reflect—what wave energy does when it hits a new material and bounces back

_____

_____

visible light waves—light waves that humans can see

_____

_____

wavelength—the length of one complete cycle of a wave

_____

_____

waves—a way that energy moves from place to place

_____

_____

Name: _____

Visible Light

All electromagnetic waves are light waves, but we can't see them all. The wavelengths in the electromagnetic spectrum that humans can see are called **visible light waves**. The rest of the wavelengths are too long or too short for our eyes to detect.

When we see light from the Sun or a light bulb, the light appears to be white. It is actually different wavelengths of visible light mixed together. When these wavelengths are separated, we see each as a different color.

You probably learned the names of these colors when you learned about rainbows: red, orange, yellow, green, blue, and violet. This is the order of the colors' wavelengths— red has the shortest wavelength, and violet has longest.

How do we see colors? We are actually seeing reflected light when we see things around us. When light hits an object, the object **absorbs** some wavelengths of light and **reflects** others. When you look at a red apple, red light waves are reflected and reach your eyes, while the surface of the apple absorbs the other colors.

Some animals can sense more wavelengths than we can. Bees and many other insects can detect ultraviolet light, which helps them find nectar in flowers. Did you know that bees can't see red or orange? Their vision starts just before the orange wavelength. And some snakes can sense infrared waves, which they use to find the warm bodies of their prey.

1. Light wavelengths that we can see are called _____.
      a. electromagnetic waves   **b.** ultraviolet light waves   **c.** visible light waves

2. The color _____ has the shortest wavelength and the color

   _____ has the longest wavelength.

3. How do we see color? Explain and give an example.

   _____

   _____

   _____

Name: _____

How We Use Electromagnetic Waves

We use the energy in electromagnetic waves to do work for us.

Radio waves have the longest wavelengths in the spectrum. They are used to send television and radio signals. Scientists use radio telescopes to study faraway things, such as planets and comets. Spacecraft send messages back to Earth via radio waves.

Microwaves are used to send cell phone and Wi-Fi signals. In a microwave oven, these waves cause water and fat molecules to vibrate, which makes the food hot.

Short **infrared waves** send signals from a remote control to a TV. We feel longer infrared waves as heat. Anything warm—stars, fire, light bulbs, and bodies—gives off infrared waves. We can't see these waves, but "thermal imaging" cameras can sense them and give us images.

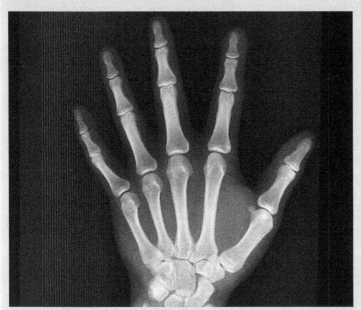

Visible light waves are the only electromagnetic waves we can see.

Ultraviolet light (UV) is part of sunlight, and we need to absorb some so our bodies can make vitamin D. But too much UV light can cause sunburns and skin cancer. That's why we need sunscreen.

X-rays pass through human tissues, but not as much through bones, so they help us see inside the human body. We also use X-rays for security to help us "see" what is inside luggage and packages.

Gamma rays have the smallest wavelengths and the most energy of any electromagnetic waves that we know of. They can kill living cells, so they are used (very carefully) to treat cancer. They are also used to kill germs on medical instruments and food.

1. The longest waves in the electromagnetic spectrum are _____.
   a. radio waves
   b. visible light rays
   c. gamma rays

2. Human eyes can only sense _____ light waves.

3. Name two ways we use electromagnetic waves to do work for us.

   _____

   _____

Name: _____

Wave Amplitude—Part 1

Waves make patterns as they travel. A **wave diagram** is like a picture of the wave's pattern at one point in time.

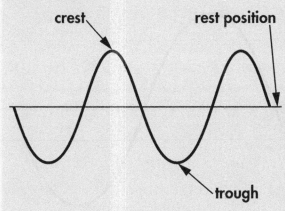

A wave diagram starts with a horizontal line called the **rest position**. This line represents where the particles will be when they are still (not moving) and no energy is being transferred.

The wave is drawn as a wavy line that goes above and below the rest position. This shows the movement of the particles.

The top of each wave (above the line) is called the **crest**, and the bottom (below the line) is called the **trough**.

Amplitude is a measure of how much energy a wave carries. Amplitude is measured from the rest position, either up to the crest or down to the trough of a wave.

Amplitude tells us about the amount of energy in a wave. The higher the crests and the lower the troughs, the more energy a wave has.

If you add more energy to a wave, its amplitude will increase.

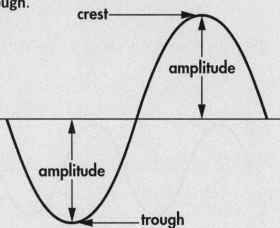

Example: In a sound wave, the amplitude tells how loud the sound is. When you turn up the volume on a TV, you are increasing the amplitude of the sound waves.

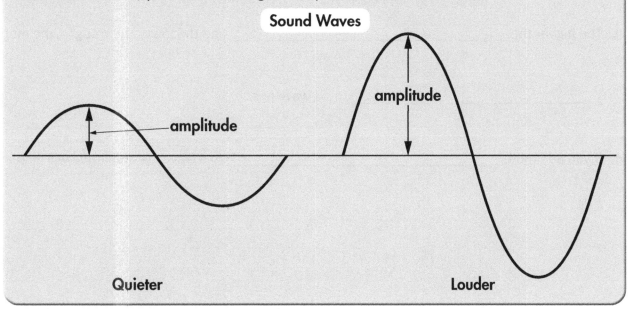

Sound Waves

Quieter   Louder

Name: _____

Wave Amplitude—Part 2

1. Label the *rest position*. Then, label one *crest*, and one *trough*. Use arrows to draw and label two measures of *amplitude.*

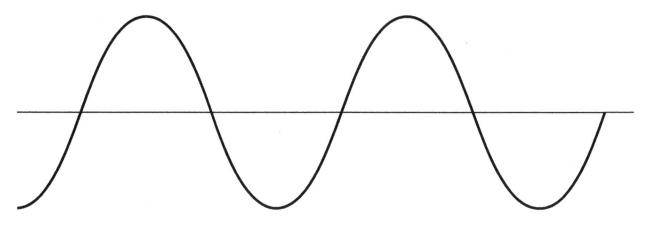

2. Circle the wave that has greater amplitude.

    a.   b.

3. The higher the _____ and the lower the troughs, the more

_____ a wave has.

4. If you add more _____ to a wave, its amplitude will increase.

Name: _____

Wavelength and Frequency

The **wavelength** of a wave is the length of one complete cycle of a wave. Wavelength is measured between two crests or troughs.

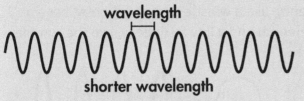

shorter wavelength

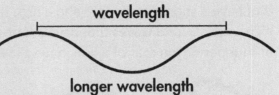

longer wavelength

Wave frequency is the number of waves that pass a fixed point in one second. The more waves that go by, the greater the frequency of the wave. A high-frequency wave has more energy than a low-frequency wave.

high frequency

low frequency

Wavelength and Frequency Are Related

A wave with a shorter wavelength has a higher frequency. A wave with a longer wavelength has a lower frequency.

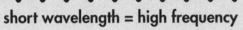

short wavelength = high frequency

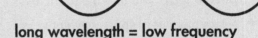

long wavelength = low frequency

1. _____ is a measure of one complete cycle of a wave.

    a. Wave frequency   **b.** Wavelength

2. _____ is the number of waves that pass a fixed point in one second.

    a. Wave frequency   **b.** Wavelength

3. Draw a low-frequency wave and a high-frequency wave. Label each diagram.

4. Circle the illustration below that shows the wave with more energy.

    a.   **b.**

Explain your choice. _____

_____

Name: _____

Sound Waves and Light Waves

Sound Waves

The wavelength and frequency of sound waves tell us about the **pitch** of the sound. Sound waves that have a short wavelength and a high frequency, like a whistle or a crying baby, have a high pitch. Sound waves that have a long wavelength and a low frequency, like the rumble of thunder or the roar of a lion, have a low pitch.

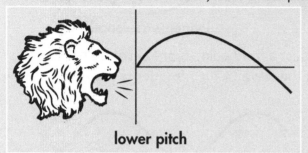
lower pitch

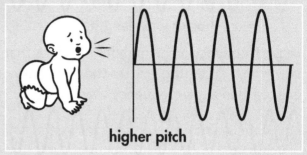
higher pitch

Light Waves

The wavelength and frequency of a light wave tells us what kind of wave it is.

➡ Radio waves have very long wavelengths and low frequencies.

➡ X-rays have very short wavelengths and high frequencies.

➡ The wavelengths of light that we can see lie somewhere in the middle.

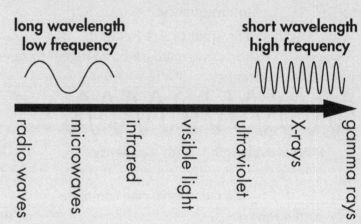

long wavelength low frequency

short wavelength high frequency

radio waves — microwaves — infrared — visible light — ultraviolet — X-rays — gamma rays

1. Which sound has a low *pitch* and a low *frequency*?
   a. a whistle   **b.** thunder   **c.** a crying baby

2. Why does the sound of thunder have a low pitch?

   _____

3. Which light waves have the lowest frequency?

   _____

4. What is the difference between *pitch* and *volume*?

   _____ is the loudness or quietness of a sound.

   _____ is the highness or lowness of a sound.

5. What does the wavelength and wave frequency of a light wave tell us?

   _____

   _____

Name: _____

Word Study—Measuring Waves

Directions: Read the words and their definitions. Then, use the words to label the wave diagram.

amplitude—a measure of the energy a wave carries measured from the wave's rest position to the crest or trough of the wave.

crest—highest point of a transverse wave

rest position—where the particles stay when there is no wave

trough—lowest point of a transverse wave

wavelength—the length of one complete cycle of a wave measured from the crest of one wave to the crest of the wave next to it.

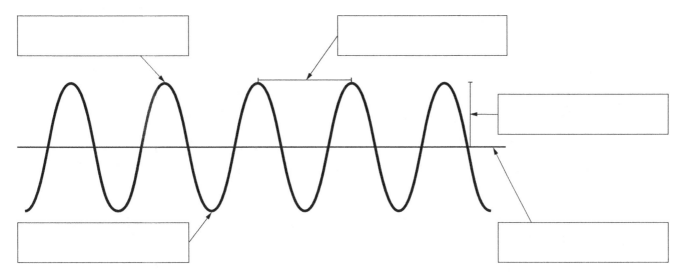

Directions: The diagram below shows the different things waves can do when they meet a new material. Read the words and their definitions. Then, write each word on the correct arrow on the diagram.

absorbed—when wave energy transfers some of its energy into a material

reflected—when wave energy hits a new material and bounces back

transmitted—when wave energy passes through a material

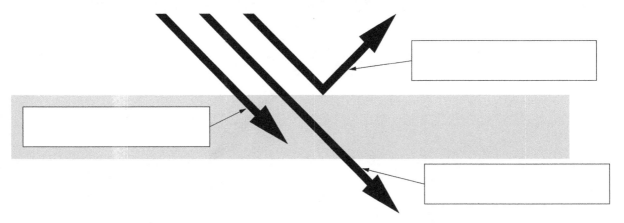

Name: _____

Wave Behavior

Waves are always moving around us. What happens when they run into things? All waves, whether they are sound waves, light waves, or ocean waves, can do three things when they interact with matter: *transmit, absorb,* or *reflect.*

Transmit

When a wave's energy passes through something, we say it **transmits** through the material.

> **Example:** Light waves transmit through clear glass windows—that is why you can see what is on the other side.

Absorb

A wave can transfer some its energy to the material it goes into. We say that the energy is **absorbed** by the medium.

> **Example 1:** When light waves hit your skin, their energy can cause your molecules to start vibrating—we feel that vibration as warmth. Our skin *absorbs* some of the energy from the light waves.

> **Example 2:** A room with carpet may seem quieter than a room with a tile floor because soft materials, like carpet, can absorb some sound waves.

Reflect

When a wave meets something that does not absorb all its energy, some of the energy can **reflect**, or bounce off, and change direction. All kinds of waves can be reflected:

> **Example 1:** The reason you can see yourself in a mirror is that light waves are reflected off of the surface of the mirror.

> **Example 2:** When a water wave hits the wall of a pool, it bounces back in the opposite direction.

> **Example 3:** When sound waves reflect, what do you hear? Echoes!

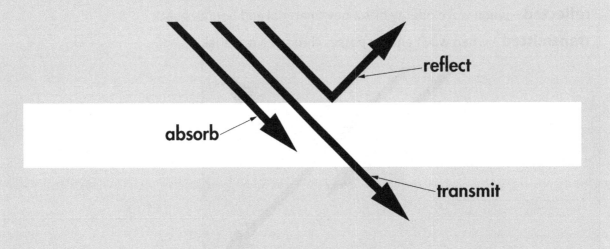

Name: _____

Wave Behavior *(cont.)*

Directions: For each example, choose the wave behavior that is causing the stated effect. Circle *absorbed*, *reflected*, or *transmitted*.

---

1 Sunlight warms the sand.

Light waves are being _____.

absorbed   reflected   transmitted

---

2 A bat makes a noise and listens for it to bounce back to find its prey.

Sound waves are being _____.

absorbed   reflected   transmitted

---

3 Snow glitters in the sunshine.

Light waves are being _____.

absorbed   reflected   transmitted

---

4 Thunder can be heard, even when you are indoors.

Sound waves are being _____.

absorbed   reflected   transmitted

---

5 A person screams into a pillow so no one will hear the sound.

Sound waves are being _____.

absorbed   reflected   transmitted

---

6 You wave at your friend through a window, and your friend waves back.

Light waves are being _____.   **absorbed   reflected   transmitted**

Name: _____

Mechanical and Electromagnetic Waves

Directions: Use the information provided below (and on other pages in the unit if needed) to answer the questions for each type of wave to complete the table below.

- All waves transport energy but not matter.
- Mechanical waves can only travel through matter.
- Electromagnetic waves can travel through both matter and empty space.
- All waves can be described by their properties: amplitude, wavelength, and frequency.
- All waves can be absorbed, reflected, and transmitted.
- Mechanical waves can be either transverse or longitudinal.
- Electromagnetic waves are only transverse.

	Ocean Wave	Sound Wave	Visible Light Wave
Is it electromagnetic or mechanical?			
Is it transverse or longitudinal?			
Does it require a medium?			
Does it transport energy?			
Does it transport matter?			
Does it absorb, reflect, and transmit?			
Does it have a wavelength and a frequency?			
Does it have an amplitude?			

Name: _____

Wave Activity

Directions: Look carefully at the four different waves. Answer each question by circling the letter of the wave.

a.  b.  c. 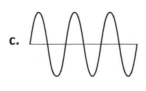 d.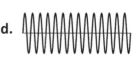

1.	Which wave has the shortest wavelength?	a	b	c	d
2.	Which wave has the highest frequency?	a	b	c	d
3.	Which wave has the highest amplitude?	a	b	c	d
4.	If these are sound waves, which is the loudest?	a	b	c	d
5.	If these are sound waves, which has the lowest pitch?	a	b	c	d

Directions: Draw each wave in a box below.

6 Draw a wave with a short wavelength and high amplitude.	**7** Draw a wave with a low frequency and high amplitude.
8 Draw a wave with a long wavelength and low amplitude.	**9** Draw a quiet, high-pitched sound wave.

Name: _____

Kinetic Energy and Potential Energy

How did you get to school today? Did you ride in a bus or a car? Did you ride your bike or walk? Whichever way you traveled, you used **energy**.

Energy is the ability to do work. It's what makes things change or move. We use energy to do things for us all the time. Energy turns on the lights, heats our food, and plays our music. Your body uses energy to think, move, and grow.

Energy can be divided into two main types: kinetic energy and potential energy.

Kinetic energy is *moving* energy. It can be moving energy of any kind—the motion of large objects we can see, such as bikes and balls, and small things we can't see, such as atoms and electrons. Atoms, the tiny building blocks all things are made of, and their parts are always in motion. Forces such as electricity and magnetism come from the motion of atomic particles.

We experience kinetic energy all the time. A car traveling down the street has kinetic energy, as does a light bulb shining or our friend's voice calling to us.

Potential energy is *stored* energy. An object with potential energy isn't working, but it has the *potential* (the ability) to do work.

Imagine a man on a bike at the top of a hill. He has potential, or *saved*, energy. If he rolls down the hill, the movement will change the potential energy into kinetic energy.

The food you eat also has potential energy. When you eat food, you turn it into kinetic energy to help you live, think, move, and grow. Potential energy can be transformed, or changed, into kinetic energy.

1. The two main forms of energy are _____ and _____.

2. *Potential energy* is _____ energy.

3. *Kinetic energy* is _____ energy.

4. For each example, circle *kinetic* or *potential*.

    - a bowling ball rolling   **kinetic   potential**

    - an airplane waiting to go down a runway   **kinetic   potential**

    - a doorbell ringing   **kinetic   potential**

    - magnets pulling toward each other   **kinetic   potential**

    - a child sitting at the top of a slide   **kinetic   potential**

Name: _____

Word Study—Energy

Directions: Write each vocabulary word next to its definition in the chart.

Word Bank

energy transfer	kinetic energy	potential energy
energy transformation	mass	speed
gravitational	mechanical energy	thermal energy

	Word	Definition
1		energy moving from one object to another
2		heat energy
3		the energy of moving things
4		the ability of an object to do work by applying force to one object to allow it to "move" another object
5		stored or saved energy
6		how fast an object is moving
7		the amount of matter in an object
8		caused by gravity
9		energy changing from one form to another

Name: _____

Energy Transformation

Try this: Rub your hands together quickly until they feel warm.

Did you create energy? No! Energy cannot be created or destroyed, but it can be changed into different forms. You just changed **mechanical energy** (rubbing your hands) into **thermal energy** (heat). This is called **energy transformation**.

You see and experience energy transformation all the time.

➡ Where did you get the energy to rub your hands together? The food you eat has chemical energy stored in its molecules. When you eat, your body transforms some of the chemical energy in food into heat energy. This allows you to move.

➡ When you turn on a computer, electrical energy is transformed into sound and light energy. This allows you to play a game.

➡ When fireworks explode, the chemical energy is transformed into light, heat, and sound.

Try this: Pick up a pencil and hold it out in front of you.

Gravity is pulling on it, so it has the *potential* to move. The higher you hold it, the more stored energy it has! The pencil has **gravitational potential energy**. What happens when you let go? The pencil's gravitational potential energy transforms into kinetic energy as it falls.

1. When you rub your hands together, mechanical energy is transformed into heat (thermal) energy. What other kind of energy do you notice?
   a. light
   b. sound
   c. chemical

2. Energy *cannot* be _____ or _____.

3. When wood burns, the chemical energy in the wood is transformed into what other kinds of energy?

   _____

   _____

   _____

Name: _____

Energy Transfer

Try this: Place a pencil on your desk. Push the pencil a little with your finger. What happens? The pencil moves! Why? It happens because of **energy transfer**.

Kinetic (moving) energy can be transferred directly from one object to another.

- ➡ When you pushed the pencil, your energy was transferred from your finger to the pencil, causing it to move.

- ➡ A piano player transfers kinetic energy to the piano keys when he plays.

- ➡ When a softball player hits, she transfers energy from her body to the bat and then the bat transfers that energy to the ball.

The amount of mechanical kinetic energy something has depends on its **mass** (how big it is) and its **speed** (how fast it is moving).

The heavier something is, the more kinetic energy it has. Imagine a Ping-Pong™ ball and a bowling ball rolling down a bowling lane at the same speed. Which has more kinetic energy? The bowling ball has more energy because it is heavier. When the balls hit the pins, their kinetic energy will be transferred to the pins. Because the bowling ball has more mass, it will hit the pins with more energy.

The faster something is moving, the more kinetic energy it has. Imagine two cars with the same mass. One is traveling at 10 miles per hour and the other is traveling at 50 mph. Which car has more kinetic energy? The one that is traveling faster has more kinetic energy. This means that if it hits something, it will transfer more energy and cause more damage. This is why it is important for drivers to obey speed limits!

1. *Energy transfer* is _____.
   a. when energy changes forms from potential to kinetic
   b. when energy travels in long and short waves
   c. when energy passes from one thing to another

2. Heavier moving things have   **more**   **less**   kinetic energy than lighter moving things.

3. The _____ or heavier something is, the more kinetic energy it has.

4. A car traveling fast could be more dangerous than one traveling slowly. Why?

_____

_____

Name: _____

Energy Activities

Kinetic energy is *moving* energy. Moving energy can be big, such as a moving car. It can also be small, such as the motion of particles that make heat, or the motion of waves that make light and sound.

Potential energy is *stored* or *saved* energy. An object with potential energy isn't doing work, but it has the *potential* to do work.

Directions: Write *potential* or *kinetic* in each sentence.

1. A ball sitting still on the ground has _____ energy.

   A ball rolling along the ground has _____ energy.

2. Water falling in a waterfall has _____ energy.

   Water in a cup has _____ energy.

3. Burning wood has _____ energy.

   Wood in a woodpile has _____ energy.

4. A cookie has _____ energy.

   When we eat a cookie, we transform it into _____ energy.

Directions: Draw and label an example of each kind of energy.

Kinetic		Potential
5 mechanical	**7** light	**9** chemical
6 thermal	**8** sound	**10** gravitational

Name: _____

Energy Transformations

Directions: Use the Word Bank. For each energy transformation, write the energy form that goes in and the energy form that comes out. The first one has been done for you. ***Note:*** Some words will be used more than once.

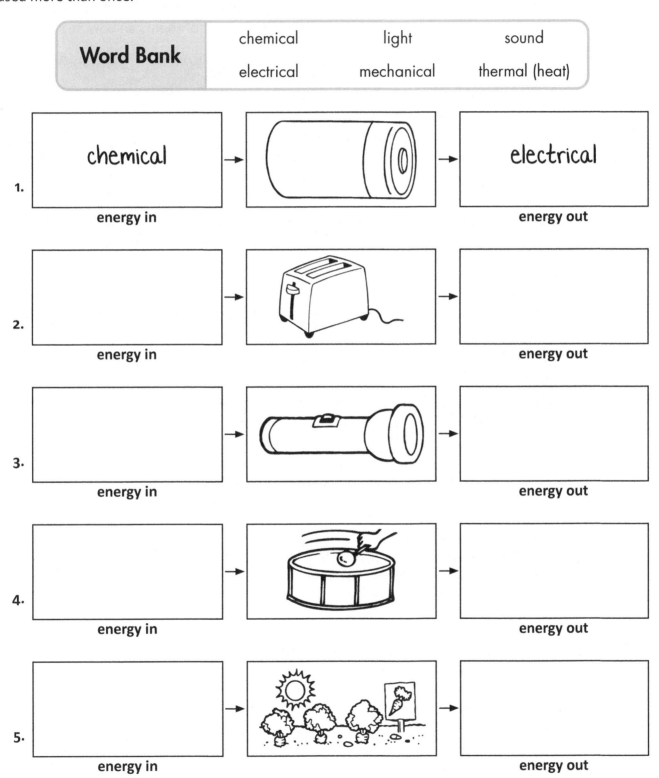

Word Bank

chemical   light   sound

electrical   mechanical   thermal (heat)

1. chemical → electrical
   energy in   energy out

2. energy in   energy out

3. energy in   energy out

4. energy in   energy out

5. energy in   energy out

Name: _____

Cells

What are you made of? You can see or feel many of your body parts—skin, eyes, hair, blood, bones, muscles—but what are those parts made of? All living things, from bacteria to plants to animals, are made of the same building blocks: **cells**. You are made of trillions of cells, but you can't see any of them. Cells are so small that most of them can only be seen through a microscope.

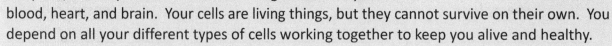

All living organisms are made of one or more cells. Some living things, such as bacteria, are **unicellular**. This means that these living things are made up of one cell that can do everything the organism needs. Other living things are **multicellular**, meaning that they are made of more than one cell. You have over 200 different kinds of cells in your body that make up different tissues and organs such as your blood, heart, and brain. Your cells are living things, but they cannot survive on their own. You depend on all your different types of cells working together to keep you alive and healthy.

People used to think that living things could come from nonliving things. They saw fleas in their houses and thought that the fleas came from dust. But now we know that living cells can only come from the same kinds of living cells, so fleas can *only* come from other fleas.

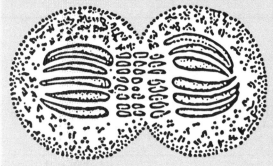

Cells make more cells like themselves through **cell division**. Each cell contains information in its **DNA** that is like a recipe for building an identical organism like itself. DNA is passed on to new cells during cell division, so each kind of cell can divide into more cells like itself. When a skin cell divides, it uses the portion of the DNA for skin cells, *not* bone cells or blood cells.

1. Which of the following is *not* true?
   a. All living things on Earth are made of cells.
   b. Most cells are too small to see without a microscope.
   c. Skin cells can divide to create blood cells.

2. All _____ _____ are made of one or more cells.

3. A long time ago, people saw mushrooms growing from dirt and thought that the dirt had turned into mushrooms. How do we know now that dirt does not turn into mushrooms?

   _____

   _____

   _____

Name: _____

Word Study—Human Cells

Directions: Fill in the graphic organizer for the term *cells*.

Definition	Word used correctly in a sentence
Example or details	**Picture**

Cells

Directions: Write a meaningful sentence to help you remember each vocabulary word related to *cells*.

1. **cell division**—the process in which a cell splits into two or more cells

   _____

2. **DNA**—molecules in a cell that carry information to control the functions of the cell

   _____

3. **function**—what something does or is used for

   _____

4. **multicellular**—an organism made of more than one cell

   _____

5. **unicellular**—an organism consisting of just one cell

   _____

Name: _____

Cell Structure and Function

There are many different kinds of cells in your body. These cells have different shapes and sizes depending on their **function**, or the job they do. Nerve cells are long and skinny because they carry signals from one part of your body to another. Red blood cells are small, round, and flexible so they can squeeze through the smallest parts of your circulatory system. Skin cells are shaped so they can fit together tightly and form a barrier to protect your body.

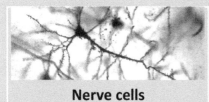
Nerve cells

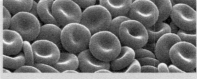
Red blood cells

Skin cells

The basic parts of your cells, however, are the same no matter what the cell's function is in your body:

➡ The outside of a cell is called the **cell membrane**. It surrounds the cell and holds it together. The cell membrane controls what moves into and out of the cell.

➡ All cells contain **cytoplasm**, which is like a clear, gooey gel. The cytoplasm is contained by the cell membrane and gives the cell its shape, like the shape of water in a water balloon. The cytoplasm has chemicals in it called **enzymes** that break down nutrients and other substances so the cell can use them.

➡ **Organelles** are parts of a cell that float in the cytoplasm. Each organelle has a job to do. The organelles in a cell work together to keep the cell alive. All cells have organelles, but they don't all have the same kinds.

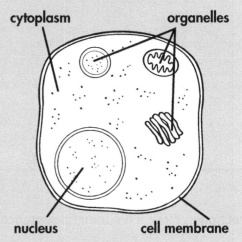

The biggest organelle in your cells is the **nucleus**. It's like the brain of the cell—it directs all the cell's activities. The nucleus also contains the DNA that is the information for making more cells.

All the organelles in a cell work together like a little factory to produce energy, make fats and proteins, and get rid of waste for the cell.

1. Which part of a cell controls its activities?
   a. membrane　　　　　　**b.** nucleus　　　　　　**c.** cytoplasm

2. A cell's size and shape are related to its _____.

3. What are the two jobs of a cell's membrane?

_____

_____

Name: _____

Animal Cell

Directions: Use the words in the Word Bank to label the parts of the animal cell. Then describe what each part does.

Word Bank   cell membrane   cytoplasm   nucleus   organelles

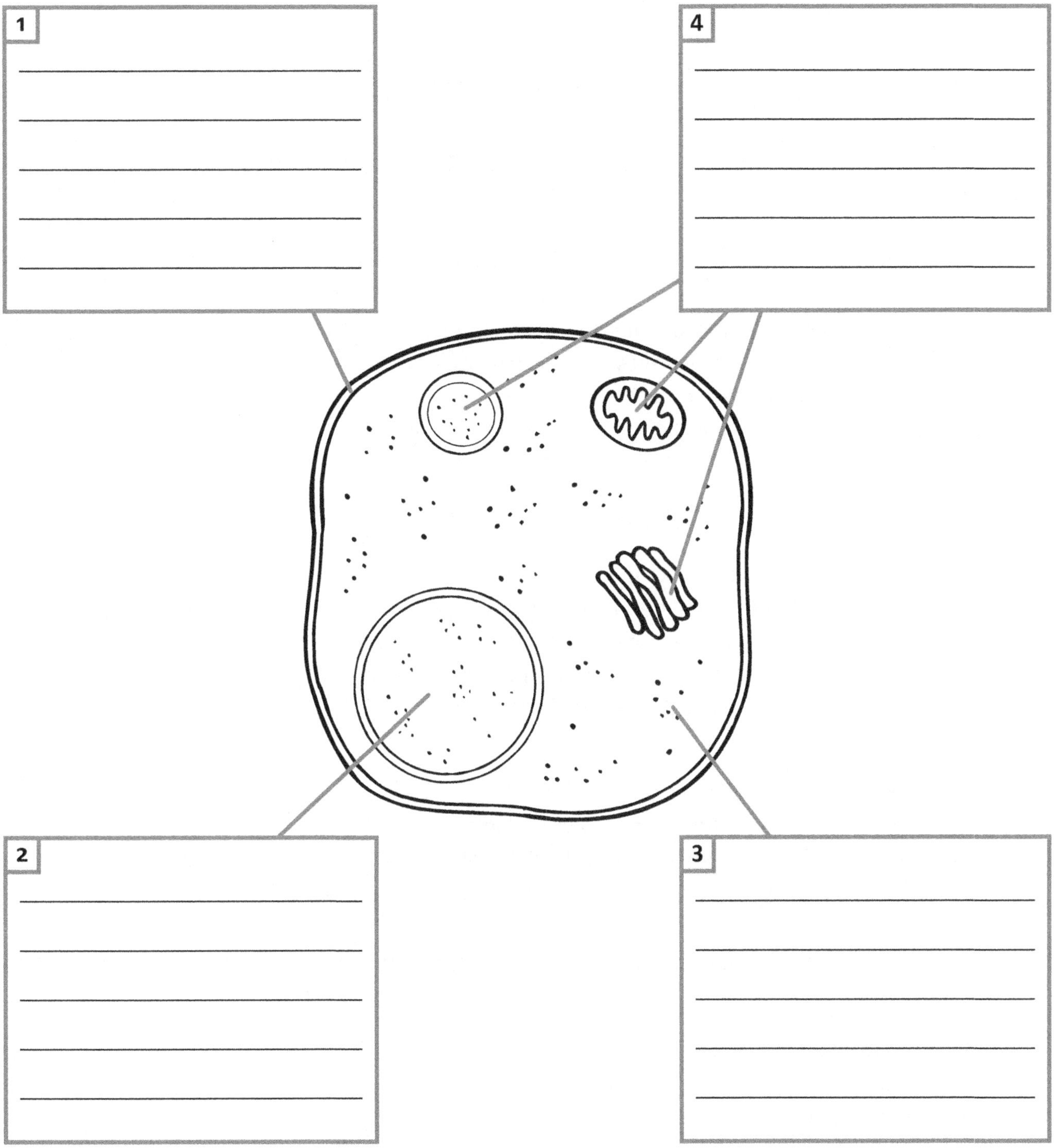

1
_____
_____
_____
_____

4
_____
_____
_____
_____

2
_____
_____
_____
_____

3
_____
_____
_____
_____

Name: _____

Cell Division in Your Body

Cell division is when a cell splits apart, making copies of itself. Cell division happens in your body all the time—about two trillion of your cells divide every day! Most of the cell division in your body is **mitosis**, when a cell splits into two exact copies of itself. Your cells divide by mitosis for three main reasons: growth, maintenance, and repair.

Growth

How does your body grow? Does each cell get bigger? No. You grow because your cells divide to make more and more cells—more bone cells to make your bones bigger, more muscle cells to make your muscles bigger, and so on.

Maintenance

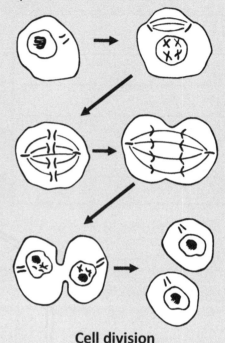

Cell division

Every day, about 25 billion of your cells die. Believe it or not, this keeps your body healthy! For example, every day, millions of your old skin cells shed (fall off). Skin cells at the bottom of your outer layers of skin are constantly dividing to make new cells, which slowly work their way to the top. In this way, your skin is constantly replacing itself, keeping it healthy. Like the cells of your skin, cells in your hair, fingernails, taste buds, and the protective lining of your stomach all get replaced constantly.

Repair

Have you ever gotten a cut or a scrape in your skin? Maybe you fell and skinned your knee. It probably got a scab, and then it healed. This is because your skin cells can divide to make new, healthy skin. If you break a bone, your bone cells can divide to make new bone cells to repair the break. Some cells can't divide to repair injury, such as the neurons in your brain, so take good care of the brain cells you have!

1. What is *mitosis*?
    a. when a cell splits into two exact copies of itself
    b. when a cell splits into two different kinds of cells

2. What are three main reasons your cells divide? Give an example for each reason.

    Reason 1: _____

    Reason 2: _____

    Reason 3: _____

3. Based on what you read about neurons in your brain, why should you wear a helmet when riding a bike or playing a sport?

    _____

    _____

Name: _____

Human Body Systems

Cells

Have you ever thought about how your body works? It all starts with **cells**. You have many different kinds of cells in your body. They work together to keep your body going.

Tissues

Cells that are similar work together in **tissues** so they can help your body:

➡ **Muscle tissues** are long, strong, and flexible like rubber bands. The cells in muscle tissues work together to pull or contract.

➡ In **epithelial tissue**, cells are packed very close together and are arranged in layers. They work together to form a barrier to protect different parts of the body.

Organs

A group of tissues that work together is called an **organ**. Some of your organs are your heart, skin, stomach, lungs, and brain. Tissues in each of your organs work together to do a job for your body:

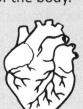

➡ The epithelial tissues of your skin protect your body.

➡ Strong muscle tissues in your heart contract to pump blood around your body.

Organ Systems

Organs are awesome, but no single organ can do all the work of your body alone! Organs work together in **organ systems**. Each organ system is necessary and works with other systems to keep your body going.

For example, the **circulatory system** works with other systems to keep your blood moving around your body. It delivers oxygen from the **respiratory system**, nutrients from the **digestive system**, as well as other substances to the cells, tissues, and organs that need them. The **circulatory system** takes carbon dioxide back to the lungs. It takes other wastes to the **excretory system**.

All the parts of your body depend on one another. Cells work together in tissues, tissues work together in organs, organs work together in organ systems, and organ systems work together in your body.

1. Which is the correct order in which your body is organized?
   a. cell ➡ tissue ➡ organ ➡ system   **c.** cell ➡ system ➡ tissue ➡ organ
   b. cell ➡ organ ➡ system ➡ tissue

2. The organs of your body work together in organ _____.

3. What do you think happens to a body when one organ system stops working? Why?

   _____

   _____

Name: _____

Your Respiratory System

Take a deep breath. Can you feel air going into your lungs? You breathe all the time, but do you know what happens each time you breathe?

First, the muscle under your lungs, called the **diaphragm**, tightens and moves down. This causes air to go in through your nose or mouth, down your **trachea**, and into your **lungs**. Your nose and mouth, trachea, and lungs are all part of your **respiratory system**.

There are two tube-like structures in your throat: the **esophagus**, which leads to your stomach, and the **trachea**, which leads to your lungs. The trachea is in the front, and the esophagus is behind it.

Your **epiglottis** is a little flap that goes up and down near the top of your trachea. This flap blocks your trachea when you swallow food and liquid to keep it from going into your lungs.

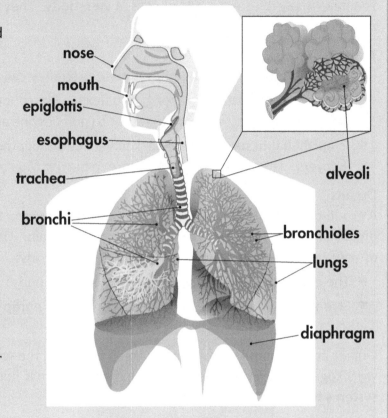

In your lungs, air goes into your **bronchi** and **bronchioles**, which look like the branches of an upside-down tree. At the end of the "branches" are tiny air sacs called **alveoli**. This is where **oxygen** from the air gets into your blood and then your heart pumps the oxygenated blood to the rest of your body. **Carbon dioxide** comes out of your blood and into the air in your lungs.

Then, your diaphragm relaxes, and the carbon-dioxide-rich air rushes out, up the trachea, and out through the nose and mouth. All this happens with every breath you take!

1. When you breathe in, how does the air travel?
    a. nose → trachea → bronchi → bronchioles → alveoli
    b. nose → bronchi → alveoli → bronchioles → trachea
    c. nose → alveoli → bronchi → bronchioles → trachea

2. In your *alveoli*, _____ from the air goes into your blood.

3. What does the *epiglottis* do?

_____

_____

Name: _____

Your Nervous System

Your brain and nerves make up your **nervous system**. Your brain is the amazing control center of your body—it's where you think and feel, learn and remember, and make decisions. It also controls many things in your body without you even knowing about it.

The brain sends and receives messages to and from the rest of the body along the **nerve cells** called **neurons**. Nerves are bundles of **neurons** (nerve cells). They carry electrical and chemical signals all over the body. Since nerves can only send signals in one direction, we need two sets:

➡ **Motor neurons** carry signals *from* the brain *to* the body.

➡ **Sensory neurons** carry signals *from* the body back *to* the brain. They tell the brain what we feel, see, hear, smell, and taste.

Try this: Wiggle your left big toe.

How does that happen? When you think about wiggling your left big toe, neurons in your brain send signals to one another. Then your brain sends a signal that travels down your **spinal cord** and along your motor neurons to the muscles around your toe, telling the muscles to move your toe. Once the muscles have done this job, sensory neurons carry a message all the way back to your brain so that you can feel your big toe moving.

Your nervous system does some things automatically without you having to think about them. It controls the important functions that keep you alive, such as breathing, digesting food, and making your heart beat. We can control some of these things some of the time—we can breathe faster or slower if we choose to. But most of the time, our nervous system handles these important things for us.

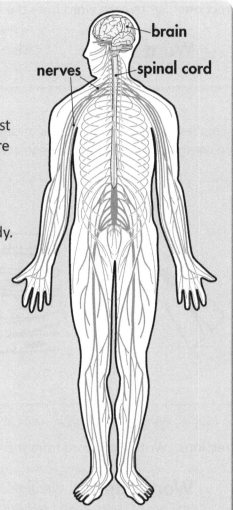

brain
nerves
spinal cord

1. When you touch your desk, which type of *neuron* carries a signal to your brain, telling it what your fingers feel?
   a. motor neuron   **b.** sensory neuron

2. _____ in your brain send signals to one another.

3. What would happen if we had to *tell* our nervous system to perform important functions like breathing, digesting, and making our heart beat?

_____

_____

Name: _____

Word Study—Human Body Systems

Directions: Write each word from the Word Bank in the correct place in the chart.

Word Bank	cells	organ	organ system	tissue

1	2	3	4
the smallest parts of all living organisms 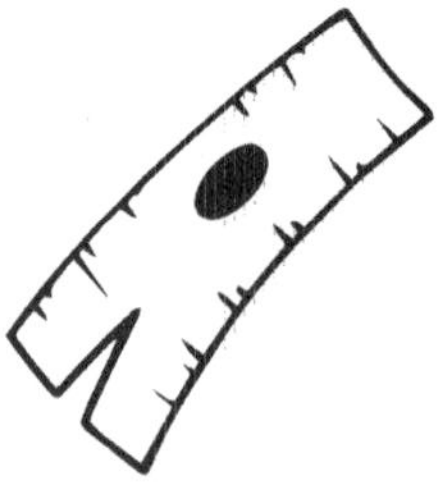	groups of cells that have similar structure 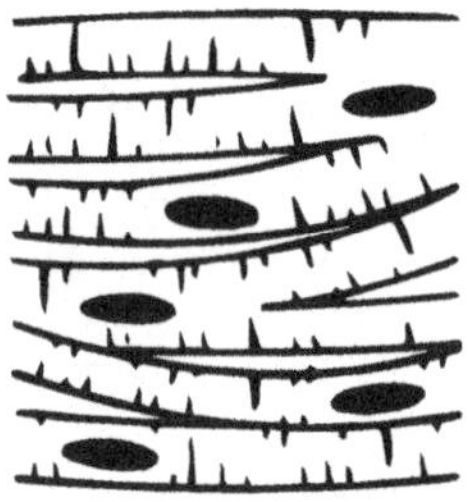	a group of tissues working together to perform a specific function 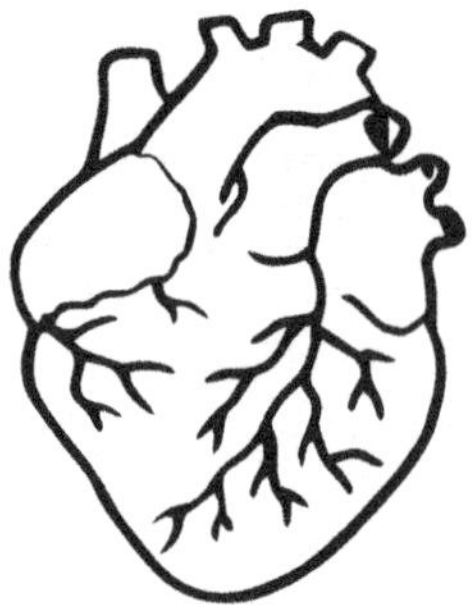	a group of organs that work together to perform one or more functions 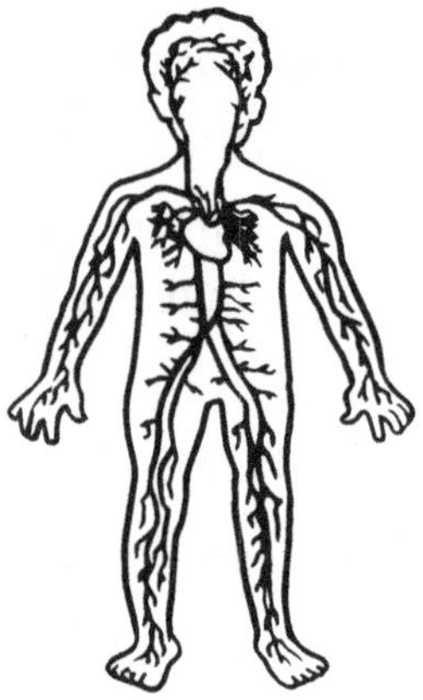

Directions: Write each word from the Word Bank in the correct place in the chart.

Word Bank	circulatory system	nervous system	respiratory system

5	6	7
the system that coordinates and controls actions in the body	the system that exchanges gasses between air and blood	the system that moves blood through the body

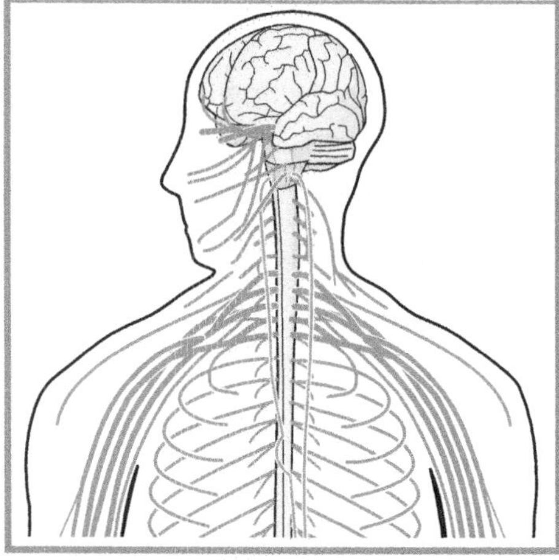

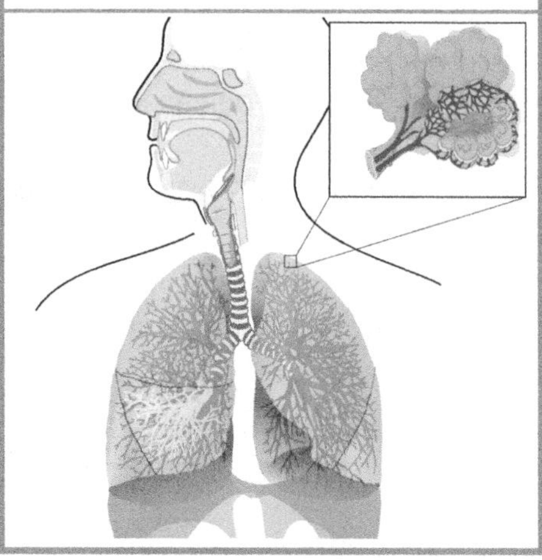

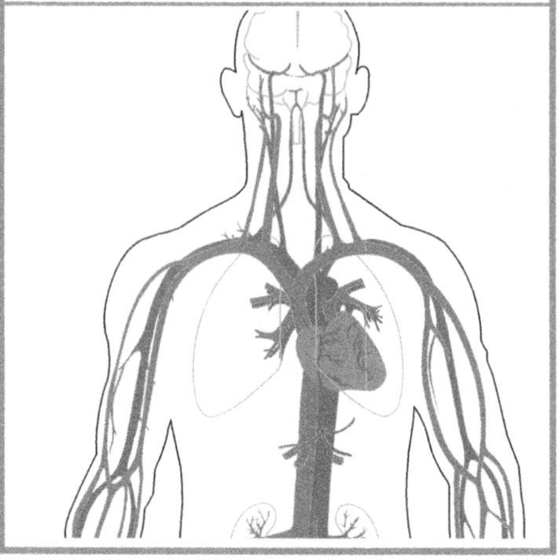

Name: _____

Review and Write—Human Body Systems

Directions: Use the words in the Word Bank to fill in the labels on the diagram and the sentences below.

1.

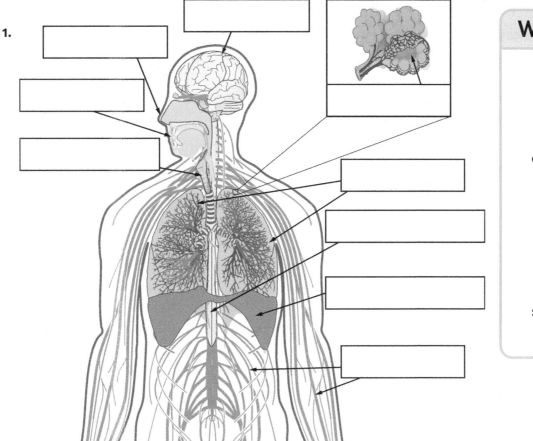

Word Bank

alveoli

blood

brain

diaphragm

lungs

mouth

neurons

nose

spinal cord

trachea

2. When you take a breath, your _____ moves down.

3. This causes air to come in through your _____

   and _____.

4. Air travels down your _____ into your _____.

5. In the _____, oxygen goes into the blood and carbon

   dioxide is removed from the _____.

6. Explain what happens in your body when you make a fist with your hand. Use all
   of the following words in your explanation: *brain, signals, motor neurons, muscles,
   sensory neurons.*

   A signal is sent to the _____

   _____

   _____

   _____

Name: _____

How Your Senses Work

Our bodies take in information about our environment by using our **senses.** Our senses allow us to respond to the world around us. This helps us to survive.

You have **sensory organs** that detect different kinds of signals from your environment. Your main sensory organs are your *eyes, ears, tongue, nose,* and *skin*. Each sensory organ has many **sensory receptors.** These are special nerve cells that can detect different kinds of energy, or **stimuli,** such as light or pressure. They turn the stimuli into signals that your nervous system can understand.

Sensory receptors send **nerve signals** that travel along your **neurons** to your **brain**. Your brain decides how important the information is and decides what to do with it.

Your brain combines information from different senses to create **memories**.

Think about it: When you eat a cookie, your brain doesn't just process information of how the cookie tastes. It combines information on taste, smell, touch, sight, and sound. So, when you look at a picture of a cookie, you see it with your eyes, but your brain can also bring up memories of tasting, touching, and smelling cookies.

Sometimes, the brain decides that a **response** is necessary. A response can be a thought or a decision, such as thinking you would like a cookie and deciding to take a bite. A response can also be an action, such as reaching for a cookie.

1. What are *sensory receptors*?
   a. nerve signals that travel to your brain
   b. specialized nerve cells that respond to stimuli
   c. kinds of energy your nerve cells can detect

2. Sensory receptors send _____ that travel along your

   _____ to your _____.

3. What are two things your brain can do with the information it receives from your senses?

   _____

   _____

   _____

Name: _____

Word Study—Senses

Directions: Write each word before its definition. Then, add an example or two in words or pictures.

Word Bank				
brain	neurons	senses		sensory receptors
memories	response	sensory organ		stimuli

	Word	Definition	Examples
1		our bodies take in information from the environment through sensory organs	
2		a part of the body containing many sensory receptors	
3		special nerves that respond to changes in the environment	
4		things or events that cause a response in a living thing	
5		the organ inside the head that controls the body's activities	
6		a group of long, thin fibers that carry information between the brain and the body	
7		information stored in the brain that can be recalled and remembered	
8		a reaction to a stimulus	

Name: _____

Your Senses at Work

Directions: Use the Word Bank to fill in the missing parts of the chart.

Word Bank   chemical   electromagnetic (light)   hearing   nose   skin

Sense	Sensory Organ	Type of Stimuli Detected
sight	eyes	
	ears	mechanical (sound waves)
touch		mechanical (pressure)
taste	tongue	
smell		chemical

Directions: For each stimulus, write which sensory organ would be able to sense it and a possible response that the brain might enact.

Sense	Sensory Organ	Possible Response
a very bright light		
a bad smell		
a sip of spoiled milk		
your friend whispering to you very quietly		
brushing up against a cactus		

Name: _____

More Than Five Senses

You have probably learned about the five senses: *sight, hearing, touch, taste,* and *smell.* But did you know that humans have more than five senses? It's true!

When we talk about our sense of "touch," we are usually talking about sensory receptors in our skin that feel pressure. But our skin can sense other stimuli, too.

➡ **Thermoreception** is the ability to feel temperature. Our skin has some sensory receptors that are activated by cold and others that are activated by heat. It is important for us to feel temperature through our skin so we don't get burned or frozen. Our brain also uses sensory information about temperature to help us warm up by shivering or help us cool off by sweating.

Our ears are the sensory organs that allow us to hear sound. But did you know that our inner ears help us with another sense as well?

➡ **Equilibrioception** is our sense of balance. It also helps us keep our eyes focused, even when our head is moving around.

Your brain uses signals from fluid in your inner ear, combined with your vision, to help you know which way is up. If you have ever spun around and around and then stopped suddenly, you know what it feels like when your *equilibrium* is off!

Try this: Tilt your head to the left and to the right. Can you keep your eyes focused on these words? Your eyes and your inner ear are working together to help you maintain your equilibrium!

➡ **Proprioception** is your sense of your own body's position and movement. Sensory receptors in your muscles and joints send information to your brain that helps you know where each part of your body is and how it is moving. That's how you can walk without having to look at your feet!

Try this: Close your eyes, and then touch a finger to your nose. Can you do it? That's your sense of proprioception telling you where both your nose and finger are relative to each other.

1. *Thermoreception* is the _____.

    a. sense of pain   **b.** sense of balance   **c.** sense of temperature

2. To keep our equilibrium, our brain uses sensory information from our

_____ and our _____.

3. What is *proprioception*? _____

Why is it important? _____

_____

Name: _____

Animal Senses

Many animals have senses of sight, hearing, taste, smell, and touch, just as humans do. Some animals can also sense things that humans cannot.

Light
Some kinds of animals can see ultraviolet light, which humans cannot see. Birds and bees use ultraviolet light to find flowers. Reindeer use ultraviolet light to find the lichens they like to eat. Some kinds of snakes can sense infrared light, which helps them find the warm bodies of their prey. Mosquitoes use infrared light to find warm-blooded bodies to bite.

Vibrations
Spiders can feel vibrations from prey trapped in their webs and can tell what kind of prey has been caught and how big it is. Spiders can also pluck their webs like violin strings, and the vibrations help them find places where the web needs to be repaired. Elephants can use their feet and trunks to *detect* vibrations traveling through the ground. They can *communicate* over long distances by making low-frequency rumbling sounds that travel quickly through the ground.

Sound
Bats can send out high-pitched sounds and then use their sense of hearing to interpret the way the sound waves bounce back to them. This is called **echolocation**, and it helps them find their prey in the dark. Dolphins also use echolocation to find food and to communicate with one another.

Touch
Cats' whiskers are specialized touch receptors. They can help tell the cat whether it will fit through a tight space, even in the dark, and can respond to vibrations in the air. Insects like ants and bees use their antennae to communicate through touch. Some antennae can also smell, taste, or hear!

Electroreception
Sharks and rays can sense electrical fields in the water. This helps them find prey in dark, murky waters and even prey buried in the sand. Bees can sense the electric fields of flowers through the tiny hairs on their bodies. This helps them tell the difference among flowers.

Magnetoception
Many animals, such as fish, turtles, butterflies, and birds, migrate or travel a long way every year. These animals can detect the magnetic field of Earth to help them find their way. Scientists aren't sure how this sense works, but they think these animals may have small amounts of magnetic material in their cells.

1. *Echolocation* is when animals _____.
   a. make a sound and use the echoes to know where things are
   b. detect low-pitched vibrations traveling through the ground
   c. sense the magnetic field of Earth to find their way around

clicks

2. What two kinds of light can animals sense that humans cannot?

   _____   _____

3. What extra sense would you like to have? _____

   Why? _____

   _____

Name: _____

Your Genes and Your Environment

What makes you who you are? And how will you change as you get older? Two main factors influence your growth and development: your **genes** and your **environment**.

You **inherit** your genes from your parents. Your genes provide instructions for how all the different cells in your body should grow. Genes determine some of your **traits**, like what color your hair and your eyes will be, how tall you might get, if you might get certain diseases, and much more.

Your environment can influence your body as well. For example, your genes might include the ability for your skin to develop freckles. But sunlight is necessary to trigger that ability, too. Without sunlight, you wouldn't have as many freckles, even though your genes say you could.

What and how much you eat, how you exercise, the stress you experience, and the climate you live in, can all affect your body. Here are a few ways that both your physical and social environment can affect your growth and development:

➡ **Nutrition:** What you eat can help determine how you grow. Your body needs enough of the right nutrients to grow to the size and shape that are coded in your genes.

➡ **Climate:** Where you live can have an impact on your body. For example, if you spend a lot of time out in the Sun without sunscreen, you risk developing skin cancer. If you live where it is cold most of the time and don't get enough sunlight, your body might not make enough vitamin D.

➡ **Family and Community:** Your relationships with the people in your life affect your development. For example, if your family reads a lot of books, that can influence you to become a strong reader as well. Your relationships with family and friends can affect the way you trust and relate to others.

➡ **Learning:** What you learn is not genetic, but your genes can influence how you learn. For example, if one or both of your parents has musical talent, you may have it as well. But if you don't *learn* to sing or play an instrument, you won't become good at making music.

1. What does *inherit* mean?
   a. environmental influence   **b.** get from your parents   **c.** growth and development

2. What are the two main factors that influence your growth and development?

   _____

   _____

3. Name one trait you inherited from your parents and one thing that you learned in your environment.

   Trait I inherited: _____

   Trait I learned in my environment: _____

Name: _____

Genotype and Phenotype

Living things pass their genes on to their offspring. Baby squirrels inherit their genes from their squirrel parents. This is why baby squirrels develop into squirrels and not into giraffes or whales. The genetic information an organism inherits from its parents is called its **genotype**.

But genotype is not the whole story. An organism's environment also has an influence on it. An organism's **phenotype** is everything we can observe about it. This includes traits influenced by its genotype *and* its environment. An organism's phenotype includes physical traits, such as size, shape, and color. It also includes behaviors, such as how a bird sings and how a beaver builds a dam.

All living things have genes and are also influenced by the environment. The interaction between genes and the environment can be complicated. But sometimes, we can easily see the influence of environmental factors in an organism's phenotype:

➡ Flamingos do not have genes that make their feathers pink. The pink color comes from the shrimp and algae that they eat. If they don't eat enough of these foods, their feathers will be white!

➡ All humans are able to learn and use language. But which language or languages you use to talk depends on what language you grew up speaking.

➡ Hydrangea plants will produce different colors of flowers depending on the soil they are growing in. Less acidic soil produces blue flowers, and more acidic soil makes the flowers pink.

➡ Himalayan rabbits have a gene for dark feet, tails, ears, and noses. This gene is only active at cold temperatures—so rabbits raised in warm temperatures are all white.

1. An organism's *genotype* is _____.
   a. everything we can observe about the organism
   b. the environment's influence on all its traits
   c. the genetic information it inherits from its parents

2. An organism's *phenotype* includes traits influenced by its _____

   and its _____.

3. Why are some flamingos pink? _____

   _____

4. Is the color of a flamingo its *genotype* or its *phenotype*?   **genotype**   **phenotype**

Name: _____

Word Study—Heredity

Directions: Review the words and definitions, and then answer the questions below.

acquired—a trait caused by environmental factors (not genes)

environment—everything around where an organism lives, including both living and nonliving things

gene—part of a cell that controls its growth; the basic unit that passes information from parent to offspring

genotype—the genes an organism inherits from its parents

inherited—a trait passed from parents to offspring

phenotype—observable characteristics of an organism, such as size, color, shape, or behavior

traits—features or characteristics of an organism

1. What does a *gene* do?

   _____

   _____

2. What are some of your *traits*?

   _____

   _____

3. What are some things in your *environment*?

   _____

   _____

4. What is the difference between an *inherited* and an *acquired* trait?

   _____

   _____

5. What is the difference between an organism's *genotype* and its *phenotype*?

   _____

   _____

   _____

Name: _____

Inherited and Acquired Traits

Inherited traits come from an organism's genes. Traits such as a person's eye color, the long neck of a giraffe, and the type of root system in a plant, are all inherited. Inherited traits *can* be passed on from parent to offspring through genes.

Acquired traits are different. Acquired traits are either learned or come from the environment. Here are some examples:

➡ a dog lifting its paw on command (learned)

➡ a broken branch on a tree (environment)

➡ the ability to learn to read (learned)

Most acquired traits *cannot* be passed on from parent to offspring.

Freckles are a combination of an inherited and an acquired trait. First, there are *inherited* genes that determine whether a person will get freckles. If the person has the inherited gene, they *can* get freckles, *if* they get enough sun. So, a person needs the correct gene and the right environment in order to get freckles.

Directions: For each trait described, choose the best answer from the options below and write the corresponding letter in the space provided.

a. inherited	**b**. acquired	**c**. a combination of inherited and acquired

1. Connor was born with pale skin. When he spends time in the sun, his skin gets darker. His skin

   color is _____.

2. All pelicans have very large beaks with pouches. Their beak shape is _____.

3. Xander hurt his knee playing soccer. Now he has a scar on his knee. His scar is _____.

4. Hannah and Helena are identical twins. Hannah eats a healthy diet and grows to 5 feet 7 inches tall.

   Helena eats an unhealthy diet and grows to 5 feet 4 inches tall. The twins' heights are _____.

5. Redbud trees have heart-shaped leaves. Their leaf shape is _____.

6. A dog was hit by a car, and doctors had to remove one of its legs. The dog's missing leg is _____.

7. Jamila speaks both English and Arabic. This trait is _____.

8. A tree grows in a place where the wind blows in one direction all the time. Its trunk bends in the

   direction of the wind. The tree's bent trunk is _____.

Name: _____

Healthy Human Habits

We know that our genes control much of how we grow and develop. But our environment and our choices make a difference, too. The interactions between our genes and our environment can be complicated, but we know for sure that some choices are good for us.

Diet
A healthy diet contributes to a healthy body. A healthy diet can make all the difference, even in people with certain genes that could make them sick or unhealthy. It's important to take in the nutrients you need to grow. Fruits, vegetables, whole grains, and lean protein should make up most of your diet. Avoid junk food as much as you can—it doesn't have the nutrients you need.

Exercise
Exercise is good for you in many ways. It encourages your brain and body to make chemicals that help you feel good. It can help you sleep better, strengthen your bones and muscles, and reduce your risk of heart disease and cancer. Try to do at least an hour of physical activity every day.

Wash Your Hands
Not everything in our environment is good for us—bacteria and viruses cause many diseases, from colds and flu to stomach illnesses. Always wash your hands with soap and water before eating, after using the bathroom, and any time you might have come into contact with germs.

Sleep
You need sleep! Getting a good night's sleep most nights can help keep you healthy. While you sleep, your brain "takes out the trash" by flushing out toxins. Adequate sleep can lower your risk of learning and attention problems. Getting enough sleep can also lower your risk of becoming overweight or developing diabetes. And you grow more while you are sleeping!

1. Your health depends completely on the genes you inherit. **True**   **False**

2. Write one healthy food you eat from each of the following groups:

   fruit: _____

   vegetable: _____

   grain: _____

   protein: _____

3. Name two healthy habits that you practice and how they help you stay healthy.

   _____

   _____

Name: _____

Reproduction

Reproduction is one of the most important parts of life. It occurs when organisms create more living things like themselves. When plants or animals reproduce, they pass their genetic information on to their **offspring**.

There are two ways that organisms can reproduce:

Asexual Reproduction

In asexual reproduction, just one parent creates offspring. The offspring will be exact genetic copies of the parent organism.

Cell division is common in single-celled organisms. A parent splits into two identical offspring. Those offspring split again and again, creating many new organisms.

➡ Bacteria are single-cell organisms that reproduce by cell division.

Fragmentation is when an organism breaks into pieces, or fragments. Each piece grows into a new organism.

➡ Flatworms, sponges, and sea stars reproduce by fragmentation.

Budding is when an organism forms a small growth called a *bud*. The bud stays attached to the parent as it develops. When the bud is mature, it breaks away from the parent and becomes a new organism.

➡ Jellyfish and corals reproduce by budding.

Sexual Reproduction

Two parents are needed for sexual reproduction. Two different cells called **gametes**, one from each parent, must join together. Each cell contains only half the genes of the parent. When the two cells join together, the offspring gets half of its genes from one parent and half from the other.

➡ Humans, most animals, and flowering plants reproduce sexually.

1. What is *reproduction*?
    a. an individual plant or animal doing what it can to survive
    b. a species dying off and becoming extinct on Earth
    c. organisms creating more living things like themselves

2. In _____ reproduction, the offspring are exact _____ copies of the parent.

3. What is the main difference between *sexual* and *asexual reproduction*?

_____

_____

Name: _____

Word Study—Reproduction

Directions: Fill in the graphic organizer for the term *reproduction*.

Definition	Word used correctly in a sentence

Reproduction

Example or details

Directions: Write a meaningful sentence to help you remember each vocabulary word related to *reproduction*.

1. **offspring**—new organisms produced by living things

   _____

2. **asexual reproduction**—reproduction by just one parent

   _____

3. **sexual reproduction**—reproduction requiring two parents

   _____

4. **territory**—an area that organisms occupy and defend

   _____

5. **pollinate**—to move pollen from flower to flower for reproduction

   _____

6. **disperse**—to move seeds away from their parent plant

   _____

7. **mate**—male and female combining cells to produce offspring

   _____

8. **gamete**—a reproductive cell with only half the genes of a normal cell

   _____

Name: _____

Animal Courtship and Competition

Most animals reproduce **sexually**. Animals must **mate** in order to pass their genes on to their offspring. A male and a female of the same species must combine their gamete cells to create offspring. There is often competition because everyone wants the best mate!

Male great frigatebird

In many species, the female chooses which male she wants for a mate. She wants to choose the male with the best genes to pass on to their offspring. Males often go to great lengths to impress females!

Females are often attracted to males with the most noticeable traits. Male peacocks have enormous, colorful tail feathers. They display these tail feathers to attract female peacocks. Magnificent frigatebird males inflate their bright-red chest pouches.

Some males sing or dance to attract and impress females. Birds, frogs, and koalas perform a mating call or song to attract mates. Some animals, such as birds of paradise, do fancy dances.

Some species build nests or other structures to attract mates. Male bowerbirds build elaborate structures out of sticks. Then, they decorate them with items, such as flowers, rocks, and even brightly colored trash.

Male stag beetles fighting

In some species, males **compete**. Whoever wins gets to mate with the females. This ensures that the genes of the fittest male are passed on. Male deer and elk, called stags, fight with their enormous antlers. Male lions, cuttlefish, and stag beetles all fight for the right to mate with the best females.

Some males establish and defend a **territory**, or area, that is under their control. Male elephant seals are enormous. They claim an area of a beach and chase away or fight any other males that come near. Then, they get to mate with all the females in their territory. Cougars, mice, and even butterflies establish and defend their territories.

1. Some males establish and defend a _____ to claim mates.
   a. territory   b. competition   c. colorful trait

2. Females want to choose the male mate with the best _____ to pass on to their

   _____.

3. Name three ways male animals may attempt to impress females.

   _____

   _____

   _____

Name: _____

Flowering-Plant Reproduction

Plants that reproduce sexually can't perform behaviors like animals do. They must rely on specialized structures and help from other sources for reproduction.

Pollination

For flowering plants to reproduce, pollen (the male gamete) must move from one flower to another flower where it can fertilize an egg cell (female gamete). Many plants rely on animals and insects to move pollen for them. Flowers use color and scent to attract pollinators. When bees, bats, or hummingbirds feed from a flower, some pollen sticks to their bodies. Then, when they go to another flower, some of the pollen falls or rubs off.

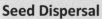

Seed Dispersal

Once pollination is complete, a seed grows. If a seed just falls off and ends up beneath the parent plant, its chances of growing and spreading aren't very good. To help, plants have developed different seed structures to help their seeds **disperse**.

➡ Some seeds are dispersed by the wind. Maple, dandelion, and cattail seeds have fluff or wings to help them float, spin, or fly in the wind. If you've ever blown the fluff off a dandelion, then you helped disperse its seeds.

➡ Some seeds use water for dispersal. Seeds growing near water often have hollow or fluffy seeds that can float down a river or a stream. The seeds land in a new place and begin to grow. Coconut palms grow on beaches, and their hollow seeds can float across oceans!

➡ Some plants are able to scatter their own seeds. Their seedpods dry out and burst, flinging the seeds in all directions.

Many plants rely on birds and other animals to disperse their seeds. Animals love to eat the sweet fruit surrounding seeds. Sometimes, they carry the fruits to a new place, and the seeds fall out while the fruits are being eaten. Some seeds are swallowed and go through the animal before being deposited in a new place. Some animals bury seeds and forget about them, allowing them to grow. Seeds with small hooks on them stick to animals' fur. Then, as the animal moves around, they fall off in new places. You may have had burrs cling to your socks.

1. *Pollination* is _____.
   a. seeds that float and travel by water
   b. moving pollen from flower to flower
   c. color and scent to attract pollinators

2. What are three ways seeds can disperse, or move away from their parent plant?

   _____   _____   _____

3. Why do you think seeds that *disperse* have a better chance of growing?

   _____

   _____

Name: _____

Which Kind of Reproduction?

Directions: For each example, determine which kind of reproduction is involved, and circle *sexual* or *asexual*.

| 1 | A female trout makes a nest in the gravel at the bottom of a shallow stream. Then, both the female and male trout deposit their reproductive gametes into the nest. |

asexual   **sexual**

| 2 | You can plant a potato in the ground, and a new, genetically identical plant will grow from it. |

asexual   **sexual**

| 3 | A *hydra* is a sea animal that looks like a plant. Hydra reproduce by budding—a bud forms on the hydra, develops into an adult, and breaks away from the parent. |

asexual   **sexual**

| 4 | Bats help wild banana plants reproduce by carrying pollen from one flower to another on their fur. The pollen from one flower joins with an egg cell in another flower to make a seed. |

asexual   **sexual**

| 5 | Bacteria reproduce by dividing into two identical cells. Some bacteria that make us sick, such as *E. coli*, can divide every 20 minutes. In just seven hours, one parent cell could divide enough times to create over a million *E. coli* bacteria! |

asexual   **sexual**

| 6 | Saddleback tortoises live in a dry environment and feed on tall cactus trees. Female saddlebacks choose to mate with males with the longest necks. This gives the best chance of their offspring having long necks so that they will be able to reach as much food as possible. |

asexual   **sexual**

| 7 | California blackworms can break apart, and each part can regenerate, or grow into a new worm. |

asexual   **sexual**

Name: _____

Ecosystems

An **ecosystem** includes all the living things in an area and the environment they live in. Forests, grasslands, tundra, deserts, and coral reefs are all examples of ecosystems. The living things in an ecosystem, such as plants and animals, are called the **biotic factors**. All the nonliving things, such as sunlight, water, air, and soil, are called the **abiotic factors**.

All living things need food, water, air, sunlight, space, and shelter to live. Within an ecosystem these **resources** can be limited, so there might not be enough for everyone.

Organisms within an ecosystem **compete** with one another for the resources they need. Sometimes, organisms of the same kind will compete for resources. If there is a limited supply of salmon in a river, grizzly bears will fight each other for the best fishing spots. Organisms of different species compete as well. Both spruce and pine trees grow in the same ecosystem. They compete for water, sunlight, and room to grow.

Organisms in an ecosystem also **depend** on one another. For example, rabbits rely on plants such as grass for food. Predators such as coyotes rely on rabbits for food. A change in the amount of grass can affect the number of rabbits, which can affect the number of coyotes. This is also true in the opposite way. More grass can mean more rabbits, which can provide more food for coyotes so their population can grow. But more coyotes eat more rabbits, which can cause the rabbit population to shrink.

Coyote

Rabbit

The grass, rabbits, and coyotes are **interdependent**. This means they depend on each other for survival. A change in the population of one will affect the others. Interdependent relationships in ecosystems can be very complicated. One change can trigger many changes throughout the entire ecosystem.

1. The living organisms in an *ecosystem* are the _____ factors.
   a. biotic   **b.** abiotic   **c.** competing

2. Organisms within an ecosystem _____ with one another for the _____ that they need.

3. Think about the interdependent relationships between grass, rabbits, and coyotes. What do you think might happen to the rabbit population if the coyotes disappeared?

   _____

   _____

   What might happen to the grass? _____

   _____

Name: _____

Word Study—Ecosystems

Directions: Fill in the graphic organizer for the term *ecosystem*.

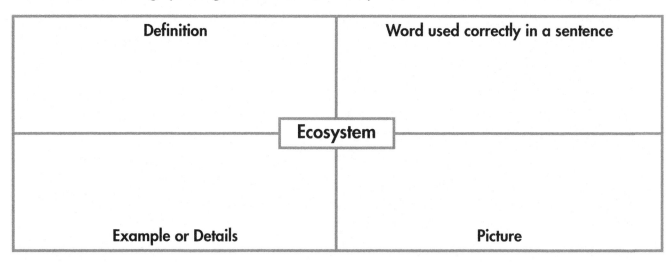

Directions: Write each term from the Word Bank before its definition. Then, add an example.

Word Bank

abiotic factors	competition	interdependence	resources
biotic factors	drivers	organism	

	Term	Definition	Examples
1		an interaction between two organisms that require the same resource	
2		the living parts of an ecosystem	
3		organisms relying on each other	
4		an animal, a plant, or another living thing	
5		substances or objects in the environment that organisms depend on	
6		the nonliving parts of an ecosystem	
7		factors that cause change in ecosystems	

Name: _____

Patterns of Interaction

Organisms live and interact with one another in an ecosystem. The three main types of interactions are *competition, predation,* and *symbiosis.*

Competition happens between organisms or species that need the same resources in an environment. Organisms of different species compete for the same resources. Lions and cheetahs both eat the same types of prey, so they compete for food. The strongest type of competition is between organisms of the same species. American robins defend a territory. They keep other robins from taking their food, water, and nesting sites.

In **predation**, one organism, the **predator**, kills and eats another organism, the **prey**. When you think of a predator, you may think of a large, fast animal like a lion or a wolf. Predators come in many sizes! Did you know that ladybugs are predators? They eat small, green bugs called aphids. Cute little meerkats love to eat scorpions. Even plants can be predators. Venus flytraps lure insects into their sticky traps and grab them!

Meerkat preying on scorpion

Symbiosis means "living together." Organisms of different species can have **symbiotic** relationships in which one or both species benefit.

➡ In mutual relationships, both species benefit. Acacia ants live in acacia trees. The tree provides food and shelter for the ants. The ants protect the acacia tree by swarming and stinging any animals that might try to eat it.

➡ Cattle egrets live with large animals such as cows, bison, and elephants. As the big animals move through grass, they disturb insects, which the cattle egrets eat. In this relationship, the cattle egret benefits and the large animals are unaffected.

➡ In **parasitism**, one species benefits and the other is harmed or even killed. If you've been bitten by a tick, then you have experienced a parasitic relationship. Ticks bite host animals and feed on their blood. The hosts get no benefit from this relationship. Ticks are parasites that can transmit illnesses such as Lyme disease to their hosts.

1. _____ can take place between organisms of the same species and organisms of different species.

2. Which of these is an example of *symbiosis*?

  a. Lions and hyenas eat the same kinds of food.

  b. Polar bears hunt and eat seals that live under sea ice.

  c. Bees pollinate plants, and plants provide food for bees.

3. What benefit do ticks get from their parasitic relationship with their hosts?

_____

_____

Name: _____

Ecosystem Interactions

Directions: For each described interaction, write *predation*, *competition*, or *symbiosis*.

| 1 | A dominant male gorilla chases younger males away from the females.

_____

| 2 | An osprey swoops down to a river and grabs a fish in its talons. It flies to the top of a nearby tree and eats the fish.

_____

| 3 | Remora fish attach themselves to the bodies of sharks. They eat the leftover bits of whatever the sharks eat. The sharks are not harmed.

_____

| 4 | In some forests, woodpeckers and squirrels both use holes and spaces in trees for nesting and storing food.

_____

| 5 | A humpback whale opens its mouth and takes in a huge gulp of water. It pushes the water out through its comb-like baleen. Then, it swallows the trapped shrimp-like crustaceans called krill.

_____

Name: _____

Change in Ecosystems

Ecosystems are changing all the time. A **driver** is an event or process that causes change in an ecosystem.

Natural disasters, such as fires, hurricanes, and volcanic eruptions, drive ecosystems. These events can kill many organisms. The abiotic factors in an ecosystem can change, too. The most dramatic example is when lava from a volcanic eruption covers the land. It destroys or covers everything that was there before. The entire area becomes a field of rock. Over time, new species will populate the lava field. A new ecosystem will arise.

Invasive species are organisms in an ecosystem that don't belong there. They can reproduce quickly and spread aggressively. They kill or crowd out **native** species. Invasive species sometimes enter an ecosystem naturally, but often, humans bring them in. The fast-growing kudzu vine was brought to the southern United States from Japan as a way to control erosion. Kudzu vines can grow a foot each day in many directions. They quickly smother native plants and trees.

Pollution from human activity can get into the air, water, and soil of an ecosystem. As plants and animals use these resources, the pollution affects them as well. Jellyfish are sea turtles' natural prey. Discarded plastic bags floating in the ocean can look just like jellyfish to a hungry turtle. A sea turtle can die from eating just one plastic bag.

Resource use is when humans gather resources from the environment. We use them to grow food, build cities, and travel in vehicles. Sometimes, to get these resources, we drive change in ecosystems. We cut down trees to get wood and to clear land for farming. Forest ecosystems change completely when these trees are removed, and most of the forest species cannot live there anymore. For example, the orangutans in Borneo are critically endangered because the forests they live in are being cut down.

1. Which *driver* of ecosystem change is not caused by humans?
   a. invasive species   **b.** pollution   **c.** natural disaster

2. A _____ is an event or _____ that causes change in an ecosystem.

3. Name one *driver* and explain how it can change an ecosystem.

_____

_____

Name: _____

Gravity and Our Solar System

Try this: Hold your pencil out in front of you over your desk. Let go. What happens? What makes the pencil fall? **Gravity** does!

Gravity is one of the fundamental forces of the universe. It is a force that pulls two bodies toward each other. You experience gravity as the force that pulls you (and your pencil) toward the center of Earth. Gravity keeps more than our bodies and our pencils on Earth. It holds everything here, including plants, animals, mountains, seas, and our atmosphere. But it's not just Earth that has gravity.

The strength of an object's gravity relates to its **mass**. Mass is the amount of matter in an object. The more mass something has, the stronger its gravitational force. You have mass, so you have gravity. But your mass is very tiny compared to Earth's mass, so your gravity doesn't have much effect here.

Earth and its Moon exert gravitational pull on each other. Because Earth weighs about 80 times more than the Moon, Earth's pull is about 80 times stronger. So why doesn't the Moon crash down to Earth? Gravitational attraction is strongest when two objects are close together. As they move farther away from each other, the pull gets weaker. Since the Moon is so far away—about 239,000 miles from Earth, it does not get pulled to us.

There is a balance between Earth's pull on the Moon, the Moon's pull on Earth, and the speed at which the Moon is moving around Earth. This keeps the Moon orbiting around Earth. If the Moon moved slower, Earth's gravity would pull it down to the surface. If the Moon moved faster, it would fly off into space!

Gravity is what holds our solar system together. The massive gravity of our Sun holds the planets in their orbits, just as the gravity of Earth holds the Moon in orbit. The Sun is by far the biggest object in our solar system. It is 1,000 times heavier than the largest planet, Jupiter, and it is more than 300,000 times heavier than Earth. In fact, over 99.8% of the mass in our solar system is in the Sun!

1. *Gravity* is _____.
   a. a force that pulls things together
   b. the amount of matter in an object
   c. how quickly an object is moving

2. Everything that has _____ has gravity.

3. Why is the Sun's gravity strong enough to keep the planets in orbit around it?

_____

_____

Name: _____

Word Study—Our Solar System

Directions: Write each term in the correct row of the chart. Then, add a drawing, an example, or a sentence showing its meaning.

Word Bank	astronomer	gravity	mass	planet

	Term	Definition	Drawing, Example, or Sentence
1		a round object that moves around a star in an unobstructed orbit	
2		a scientist who studies natural objects in space	
3		the amount of matter in an object	
4		a force that attracts two objects towards each other	

Directions: Write each term under the correct image.

Word Bank	lunar cycle	lunar eclipse	orbit	solar eclipse

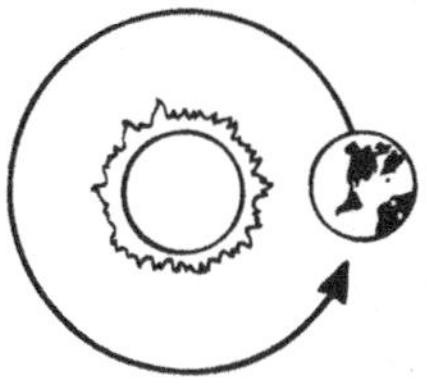

5. _____

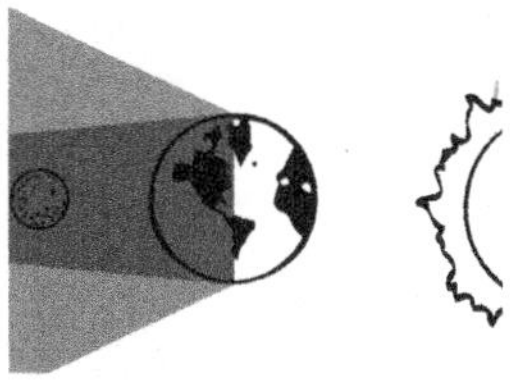

_____

6. _____

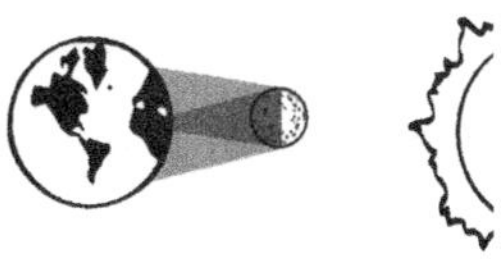

_____

7. _____

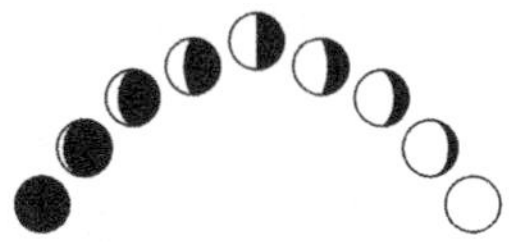

_____

8. _____

_____

Name: _____

Moon Movement

If you've ever seen a full moon shining in a dark sky, you know how bright it can appear. Where does that light come from? Does the Moon make the light? No—the light we see is sunlight *reflected* off the surface of the Moon. The Sun always shines on half of the Moon, the same way we have day and night on Earth.

As the Moon orbits around Earth, we always see the same side of the Moon. But as the Moon and Earth's positions change relative to the Sun, our view of the "daylight" part of the Moon changes. Over about 29 days, we see all the phases of the Moon that make up the **lunar cycle**. This regular and predictable pattern is caused by the changing positions of Earth and the Moon relative to the Sun.

Have you ever seen the Moon during the daytime? When the Sun and Moon are in our sky at the same time, the Moon doesn't appear as bright as it does at night. Like the phases of the Moon, the changes in when you can see the Moon in the sky are caused by the movements of the Moon and Earth.

Sometimes, the Moon comes between your part of Earth and the Sun, and you get to experience a **solar eclipse**. The Sun appears to darken as the shadow of the Moon moves across Earth. Depending on where you are, you may see a partial or total eclipse of the Sun. Not everyone on the daylight side of Earth will see a solar eclipse at the same time because the Moon's shadow is relatively small.

Solar eclipse

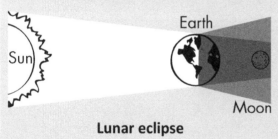

Lunar eclipse

When Earth is between the Sun and Moon, you may see a **lunar eclipse**. Everyone on the nighttime side of Earth can see a lunar eclipse when it happens because Earth's shadow is larger than the Moon. Because the movements of the Moon and Earth are regular, astronomers can predict when eclipses will happen.

1. The movements of the Moon and Earth are _____.
   a. regular and predictable   b. irregular and unpredictable

2. Over about 29 days, we see all the _____ of the Moon

   that make up the _____ _____.

3. In a *solar eclipse*, the shadow of the _____ moves across

   _____.

4. In a *lunar eclipse*, the shadow of _____ moves across the

   _____.

Name: _____

Is Pluto a Planet?

For a long time, Pluto was considered the ninth **planet** in our solar system. Then, an astronomer discovered another object, called Eris. It was similar in size to Pluto. Could it be a tenth planet? This caused great debate among **astronomers**, the scientists who study objects in space.

Astronomers worked for two years to decide what a planet actually is. In 2006, they decided that to be a planet, an object in the solar system must follow these three rules:

1. A planet must orbit the Sun.

2. A planet must be large enough that its own gravity pulls it into a round shape.

3. A planet must have "cleared its neighborhood" so there are no other bodies of larger or similar size in its orbit.

Read these facts about Pluto, and decide if it meets the definition of a planet.

➡ Pluto is round and has reddish and pale patches. It has a large glacier shaped like a heart, blue skies, mountains as high as the Rockies, and red snow!

➡ Pluto is 1,450 miles in diameter. It is smaller than Earth's Moon and half the width of the United States. Its largest moon, Charon, is so big that Pluto and Charon orbit each other like a double planet.

Pluto (lower right) and Charon (upper left)

➡ Because Pluto is smaller than Earth, its surface gravity is weaker than the surface gravity on Earth. If you weigh 100 pounds on Earth, you would weigh less than 10 pounds on Pluto.

➡ Pluto's orbit around the Sun is oval shaped and the Sun is not at the center. Pluto's orbit is tilted when compared to the eight planets orbiting the Sun.

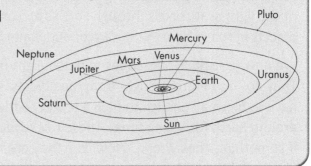

➡ Pluto shares its orbital neighborhood with lots of other objects in the Kuiper Belt, a ring of icy objects beyond Neptune.

Directions: Does Pluto follow each rule to be a planet? Look for evidence in the text. Circle *Yes* or *No* and copy your evidence from the text.

1. A planet must orbit the Sun.　　　　**Yes**　　　　**No**

   Evidence: _____

2. A planet must be large enough that its own gravity pulls it into a round shape.　　**Yes**　　**No**

   Evidence: _____

3. A planet must have "cleared its neighborhood" so there are no other bodies of larger or similar size in its orbit.　　**Yes**　　**No**

   Evidence: _____

Pluto and Charon, NASA/Johns Hopkins University Applied Physics Laboratory/Southwest Research Institute.

Name: _____

Telescopes

When you look into a clear night sky, you can usually see stars. Sometimes, you can see the Moon and even some planets. For thousands of years, people observed our universe with just their eyes. Early civilizations used the movements of the Sun, Moon, and stars in the sky to keep track of time and find their way. The night skies were also important in cultural and religious beliefs.

Reconstruction of Galileo's telescope

Then, people discovered that they could use glass lenses to magnify their view. This led to the first **telescopes**. Telescopes are instruments for viewing distant objects. Telescopes make faraway objects look bigger, brighter, and closer. Galileo was the first to use a telescope to observe objects in the night sky.

Gran Telescopio Canarias

Over time, the design of telescopes has improved. Many telescopes now use mirrors. Mirrors give a clearer view than glass lenses. Scientists and engineers are building huge telescopes to help them see very distant objects. The largest reflecting telescope on Earth is the Gran Telescopio Canarias. This massive telescope gives us views of galaxies hundreds of millions of light-years away.

But there is a problem with using a telescope on Earth. Have you ever seen a star twinkle? The star's light isn't actually getting darker and brighter. The twinkling effect comes from the bending of the light as it travels through Earth's atmosphere. We can never get a truly clear view of objects in space from the surface of our planet because we are looking through our atmosphere.

We now use **space telescopes** to detect light from stars, galaxies, and other objects in space. They do this before the light from the objects is distorted by the atmosphere. Space telescopes have to be small enough to fit in a rocket so they can be launched into space. They stay in orbit around Earth for a long time. These telescopes are very expensive and very difficult to repair if something goes wrong. However, they are important because they send us much better views of distant objects in space than even the largest telescope on the ground.

1. *Telescopes _____.*
   a. are only used to view space from Earth
   b. always use mirrors to make things look closer
   c. are instruments for viewing distant objects

2. _____ telescopes stay in _____ around Earth.

3. Why do stars appear to twinkle when we look at them from Earth?

_____

_____

#8266 Let's Get This Day Started: Science   *©Teacher Created Resources*

Name: _____

The Hydrologic Cycle

Do you ever think about where that water comes from when you drink a glass of water or take a shower? Most of the water on Earth doesn't move around much. Look at the pie chart to the right. About 97% of all the water on Earth is in the oceans. A drop of water can spend over 3,000 years in the ocean before evaporating into the air. About 2% of Earth's water is frozen in ice sheets and glaciers. This water tends to stay frozen for a long time. The oldest ice in Antarctica has been there for more than two million years! Most of the remaining 1% of Earth's water is underground. Only 0.03% of the water on Earth is fresh water in lakes, wetlands, and rivers.

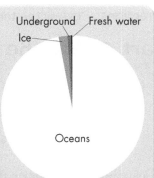

Water on Earth

Lucky for us, there is a small amount of fresh water that does move around Earth. Here is how it happens:

1. The heat of the Sun causes water on the surface of the ocean to **evaporate**. It enters the atmosphere as **water vapor**. Dense, cool air is pulled down by gravity, which forces the warmer, humid air up.

2. As water vapor moves higher, it cools and **condenses** into clouds.

3. The condensing water droplets or ice crystals in clouds get heavy. Gravity pulls **precipitation** (solid snow or liquid rain) back down to the ground or the oceans.

4. Gravity pulls water downhill in streams and rivers as **runoff**. The water returns to the ocean.

This constant cycling of water through different places and states is called the **hydrologic cycle**, also known as the water cycle.

We know that if water is moving and changing states, there has to be some **energy** involved. Where does the energy powering the hydrologic cycle come from? The energy to move water up, through evaporation, comes from the Sun. The energy to pull water down, as precipitation and runoff comes from gravity.

1. What is another name for the *Hydrologic Cycle*?
   a. Sedimentary Cycle   **b.** Water Cycle   **c.** Rock Cycle

2. Sun warms the surface of the ocean, causing water to _____, or become water vapor.
   a. condense   **b.** precipitate   **c.** evaporate

3. Where is most of the water on Earth? _____

   _____

4. Why do you think some of the ice in Antarctica has been there so long?

   _____

   _____

Name: _____

Word Study—Earth Cycles

Directions: Review the terms and their definitions. Then, use the terms to complete each passage.

Part One: The Water Cycle

> **condenses:** changes from gas to liquid
>
> **evaporates:** changes from liquid to gas
>
> **precipitation:** rain, snow, hail, etc. that falls to the ground

The Sun warms water on the surface of the ocean, and it _____. The

1

warm air and water vapor travel upward. As it cools, the water vapor _____

2

into clouds. As the ice crystals or water droplets get heavier, they fall from the clouds as

_____.

3

Part Two: Weathering and Erosion

> **erosion:** the moving of sediment
>
> **weather:** wind and water wear down rock into sediment
>
> **deposited:** when sediment settles in a new location
>
> **sediment:** small bits of broken rock

Wind, water, and ice _____ rocks and break them into small particles called

4

_____. The particles are moved by wind and water. This is called

5

_____. Finally, the sediment is _____ in a new place.

6   7

Part Three: Types of Rocks

Directions: Match each vocabulary word to its definition.

igneous _____   **a.** rocks formed from cooling lava

lava _____   **b.** rocks changed by heat and pressure

metamorphic _____   **c.** rock made of pieces of other rock

magma _____   **d.** melted rock under the surface of Earth

sedimentary _____   **e.** melted rock above the surface of Earth

Name: _____

The Rock Cycle—Heat and Pressure

Do rocks last forever? It might seem like it, but rocks are changing all the time. Most of these changes are so slow that you will never see them. Any rock on Earth can be changed into a different kind of rock through a series of processes known as the **rock cycle**. The energy that changes rocks comes from heat inside Earth and heat from the Sun.

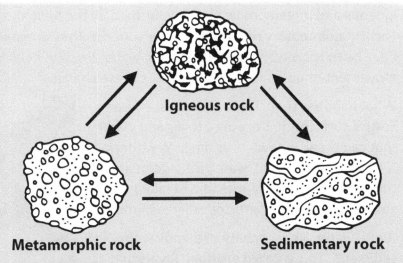

Igneous rock

Metamorphic rock

Sedimentary rock

Rocks can be created and changed by energy from Earth's interior. You know that ice can melt and change into liquid water. But did you know that rocks can melt, too? It takes very high temperatures to melt rock. Most rocks melt between 1,100° and 2,400° F. Temperatures that high are usually only found deep in Earth. For comparison, the hottest day ever recorded on the surface of Earth was 134° F.

Hot, molten rock is called **magma** when it is under the surface. When it reaches the surface, usually through a volcano, it is called **lava**. **Igneous rocks** are formed when magma cools under the surface or when lava cools and hardens on the surface.

Volcano

Rocks don't have to melt to change. Rocks can also form and change from pressure, as layers of rock press down on one another. Imagine someone put a lot of blankets over you. The more blanket layers they add, the more the layers press down on you.

Metamorphic rock

The pressure from layers of rock pushing down is strong enough to change the rocks underneath. As rocks are squeezed by pressure and heated for a long time, they change into different kinds of rocks. **Metamorphic rocks** are rocks that have been changed by heat and pressure without melting.

1. Melted rock below the surface of Earth is called _____.
   a. lava   **b.** igneous   **c.** magma

2. What kind of rock is changed by heat and pressure without melting?

   _____

3. How is *igneous rock* formed? _____

   _____

Name: _____

The Rock Cycle—Weathering and Erosion

Igneous and metamorphic rocks are formed by the heat and pressure *under* the surface of Earth. **Sedimentary rocks** start *on* the surface. They are made from smaller bits of rock that have been broken and moved by wind, water, ice, and heat. Energy from the Sun drives the movement of air and water that causes these changes.

What happens to rock when it is pushed up to Earth's surface? It is exposed to air and water that can break it down over time. **Weathering** is the process of wind, water, ice, and heat from the Sun wearing down rock and breaking it into smaller and smaller particles called **sediment**.

Sedimentary rocks

Wind, water, ice, or gravity then moves the sediment. This is called **erosion**. Rivers and glaciers carry sediment downhill. Wind blows sediment across the land.

Deposition is when the sediment settles, or is *deposited,* in a new place. It usually collects on the bottom of oceans and lakes. Often, bits of shell, dead animals, and plants are mixed in with rocks and sand in the sediment. Sedimentary rocks are formed when deposited sediment forms layers over each other and are pressed together.

Dinosaur footprint

Scientists can study the layers in sedimentary rock to learn about the distant past. They study the thickness, color, and shape of the layers. They observe the sizes of the sediment particles and any fossils embedded in the rock. Fossils can tell about ancient plants and animals as well as what the climate was like when sediment was formed. Scientists have even found dinosaur footprints in sedimentary rock!

Fossil fuels—oil, coal, and natural gas—are formed in sedimentary rock. They are the remains of plants and animals changed by heat and pressure.

1. _____ is when *sediment* settles in a new place.

    a. Weathering   **b.** Erosion   **c.** Deposition

2. What is the difference between *weathering* and *erosion*? _____

_____

3. How is *sedimentary rock* formed? _____

_____

Name: _____

Follow the Rock Activity

There are three main types of rocks formed in the rock cycle:

➡ **Igneous rock**—melted rock that cools and hardens

➡ **Sedimentary rock**—made of pieces of other rock

➡ **Metamorphic rock**—changed by heat and pressure

Rocks can change from one type to another and back again. An igneous rock could move deep underground and become a metamorphic rock. Or it could become weathered and become part of a sedimentary rock. There is more than one way to become a rock!

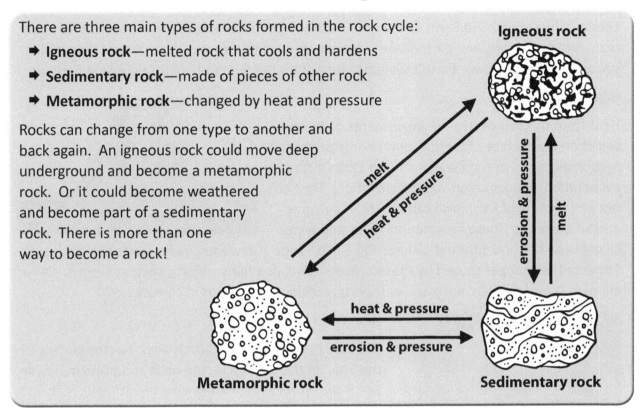

Directions: Trace each changing rock through the rock cycle diagram. Use a different-colored highlighter or colored pencil to show each path. Write an explanation of its journey. The first one has been done for you.

Example

Path ➡ metamorphic rock to igneous rock

A metamorphic rock is melted underground and becomes magma. The magma is spewed out of a volcano as lava. The lava cools and becomes igneous rock.

---

1. **Path ➡ igneous rock to sedimentary rock**

   _____

   _____

2. **Path ➡ sedimentary rock to metamorphic rock**

   _____

   _____

3. **Path ➡ metamorphic rock to sedimentary rock**

   _____

   _____

Name: _____

Energy Flow and Earth Cycles

Energy is flowing around Earth all the time. It drives powerful natural events such as lightning, tsunamis, volcanoes, and earthquakes. Where does all this energy come from? Two major sources of energy power Earth's systems: heat from the Sun and heat from inside Earth.

Heat from the Sun

Heat from the Sun causes the movements of air and water on the surface of Earth. Solar energy drives the hydrologic cycle, moving water around Earth through evaporation, condensation, and precipitation. The Sun's uneven heating of Earth also causes ocean currents and air currents. These movements of air and water create weather and different climates on Earth. They also weather and erode the landscape. Some of the changes caused by these processes happen fairly quickly, such as storms. Other changes happen slowly, such as weathering, erosion, or changes in climates.

Heat from Inside Earth

The core in the center of Earth is as hot as the surface of the Sun. In the rock cycle, the heat and pressure inside Earth causes rocks to melt or change. It melts rock into magma, which can form igneous rocks. Its heat combines with pressure to change igneous rocks into metamorphic rocks. A few of the changes caused by these processes happen quickly, such as volcanic eruptions, but most take thousands or even millions of years.

In both the water cycle and the rock cycle, matter changes states through heating and cooling:

➡ Heat from the Sun causes liquid water to become water vapor. As water vapor rises in the atmosphere, it cools. Then, it condenses into liquid.

➡ Heat inside Earth melts rock into liquid. As the liquid rock rises toward Earth's surface, it cools and becomes solid.

1. What two major sources of energy drive Earth's processes?

_____

_____

2. Heat from the Sun causes the movements of _____ and

_____ on the surface of Earth.

3. How are the rock cycle and the water cycle alike?

_____

_____

Name: _____

Inside Earth

The **core** at the center of Earth is very, very hot. It has two parts—a solid inner core and a liquid outer core. Wrapped around that hot center is a layer called the **mantle**. The inner part of the mantle close to the core is partially melted and can flow slowly. The upper part of the mantle is solid. The **crust** is the thin, rocky outer layer where we live.

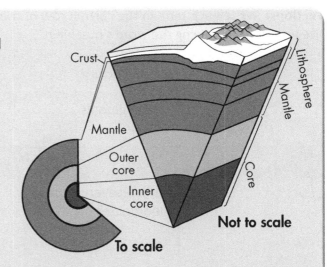

The **lithosphere** is made up of the upper mantle and the crust. Large pieces of the lithosphere, called **tectonic plates**, float on the flowing inner mantle. There are eight major plates and a lot of minor plates. Both land and oceans ride on these plates. The ocean plates are between 5 and 10 miles thick. The plates on land are about 22 miles thick.

These huge plates move very slowly but with a lot of power. They are crashing into each other, grinding along each other, and pushing each other, all in slow motion. How slow do they move? The slowest-moving plates move only one inch per year, and the fastest move about six inches per year.

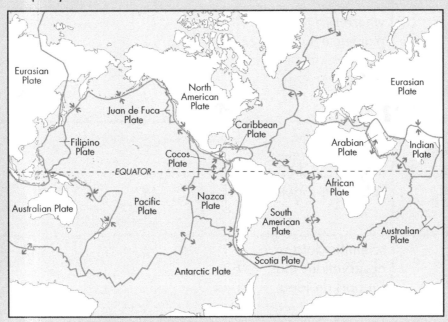

1. *Tectonic plates* are large pieces of Earth's _____.
   a. core   **b.** mantle   **c.** lithosphere

2. The _____ is the thin, rocky outer layer of Earth where we live.

3. If a plate moves two inches per year, how many inches has it moved in your lifetime so far?

_____

USGS.

Name: _____

Word Study—Plate Tectonics

Directions: Write each term in the correct row of the chart. Then, add a drawing, give an example, or write a sentence showing the word's meaning.

Word Bank			
	boundary	evidence	supercontinent
	continents	fossil	tectonic plates

	Term	Definition	Drawing, Example, or Sentence
1		Earth's seven largest landmasses	
2		giant pieces of the outer surface of Earth that float on the hot mantle underneath	
3		where two tectonic plates meet	
4		a single large landmass formed by most or all of Earth's continents together	
5		scientific data or observations that support an idea	
6		the shape of a living thing that has been preserved in rock for a very long time	

Name: _____

Tectonic Plate Boundaries

A **tectonic boundary** is where two plates meet. There are three kinds of tectonic boundaries.

➡ **Divergent boundaries** are where two plates are moving away from each other. Magma oozes or erupts from the opening between the plates and hardens into solid rock, creating new crust. In the oceans, divergent boundaries create mid-ocean ridges as plates move apart and new ocean floor is created. The mid-ocean ridges around the world are connected, forming the longest range of mountains on Earth.

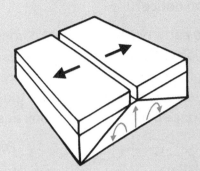

➡ **Convergent boundaries** are where two plates push into each other. In some places, the power of the two plates crashing into each other crumples the edge of one or both plates up into a mountain range. Sometimes, the stronger plate bends the other plate down into a deep trench. The rocks of the weaker plate melt, and volcanoes often form near the boundary. Earthquakes are common as the plates push on each other.

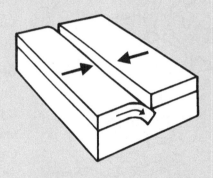

➡ **Transform boundaries** are where two plates are sliding past each other in opposite directions. They don't slide smoothly! Rocks build up friction and stick against each other, building up strength until they suddenly release and a large earthquake occurs. In a transform boundary, no magma is created, so no new crust is formed.

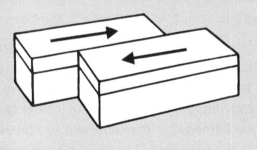

1. The place where two tectonic plates meet is called a(n) _____.
   a. earthquake   **b.** mantle   **c.** boundary

2. Write the name of each boundary type next to its definition.

   a. where two plates *push into* each other _____

   b. where two plates *slide past* each other _____

   c. where two plates *move away from* each other _____

3. How is new crust created at a divergent boundary?

   _____

   _____

Name: _____

The Biggest Changes on Earth

Take a look at the **continents** of South America and Africa. What do you notice?

In the early 1900s, a scientist named Alfred Wegener thought that they looked like giant puzzle pieces that fit together. In fact, he thought all the continents had once been joined and that they had moved apart to where they are today. Could Earth's continents all have once been one? Let's look at some of Wegener's **evidence**.

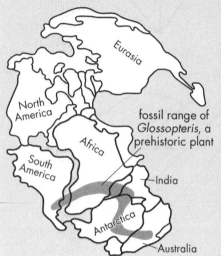

fossil range of *Glossopteris*, a prehistoric plant

Fossils: Scientists have found some of the same types of certain reptile and mammal fossils in both Africa and South America. It would have been impossible for these creatures to swim between the continents. Fossils of the same ancient plant are found on five continents, meaning that those continents must all have been joined in the past.

Geology: Identical rocks of the same kind and age can be found on both sides of the Atlantic Ocean. They must have formed in the same place and then been separated. For example, the mountains in the eastern United States and Canada match mountain ranges in Ireland, Great Britain, and Norway.

Despite all this evidence, Wegener wasn't able to convince most other scientists of his idea at the time.

Since that time scientists have gathered new evidence. Now, we know that the land we live on, as well as the oceans, float on huge **tectonic plates** over the hot inner mantle of Earth. These plates are moving very slowly—only an inch or two each year. Scientists have confirmed that the continents do move, and millions of years ago, they were joined together in a **supercontinent** called **Pangaea**. In fact, continents have moved together and apart many times over the history of Earth.

Mountain ranges

---

1. *Evidence* is _____.
   a. scientific data or observations
   b. continents joined together
   c. fossils found in two places

2. Earth's land and oceans float on _____.

3. What was *Pangaea*? _____

   Describe *Pangaea*. _____

   _____

Name: _____

Plate Tectonics Activity

Directions: Label the parts of Earth.

Word Bank	crust	inner core	lithosphere	mantle	outer core

1.

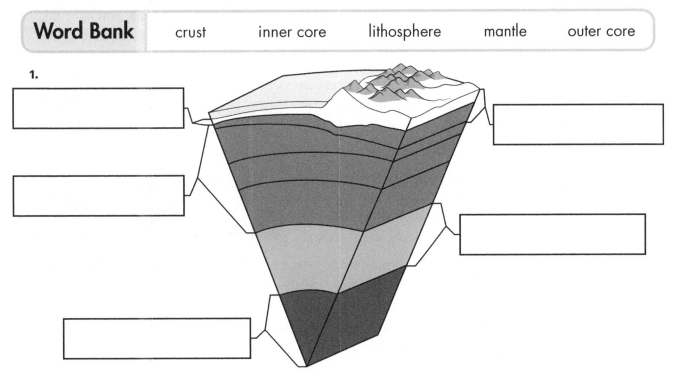

Directions: Label each type of boundary and explain how the plates move and what effects that movement creates.

2. _____
   _____
   _____

3. _____
   _____
   _____

4. _____
   _____
   _____

Name: _____

Weather or Climate?

What is the weather outside like right now? Imagine it's a summer day. In the morning, it's hot, humid, and sunny. In the afternoon, a big thunderstorm rolls in with rain, hail, and lightning. Is this *weather* or *climate*? Both weather and climate tell you about the atmosphere, which is the layer of gases around Earth.

Weather tells what is going on in the atmosphere *in a place for a short time*. Weather is temporary—the weather we experience today could be different from the weather we have tomorrow.

Every place on Earth has weather all the time, but it's not the same everywhere. For example, in one part of the world, the weather might be sunny, hot, and dry, and in another part, it might be windy and snowy.

Climate is different from weather. Climate is the *pattern of weather in a place over a long period of time*. To define an area's climate, scientists measure temperature and precipitation over at least 30 years. The measurements are not the same each year, but they do have patterns. For example, in North Dakota, it is hot and humid in the summer and very cold and snowy in the winter. The climate in Southern California has warm, dry summers and the winters are mild. These patterns repeat year to year.

1. The *atmosphere* is _____.
   a. the amount of water vapor in the air
   b. the layer of gases around Earth
   c. a pattern of weather over a long time

2. *Climate* is the _____ of weather in a place over

   _____.

3. What is the difference between *weather* and *climate*?

   _____

   _____

Name: _____

Word Study—Weather and Climate

Directions: Write the similarities and differences between *weather* and *climate* in the Venn diagram.

> **Weather:** the atmospheric conditions in one area at a particular time; day-to-day changes in temperature, precipitation, and wind
>
> **Climate:** the average weather in a place over a long time, usually defined by patterns in temperature and precipitation

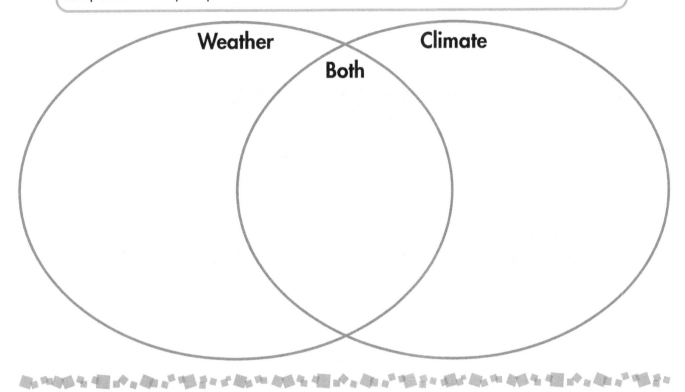

Directions: Write meaningful sentences using the vocabulary words. Try to use more than one vocabulary word in each sentence.

atmosphere: the layer of gases around Earth

forecast: a prediction or an estimate of what will happen

meteorologist: a scientist who studies the weather; a weather forecaster

equator: an imaginary line drawn around the middle of Earth that is an equal distance from the North Pole and the South Pole

current: a steady flow of ocean water or air

_____

_____

_____

_____

Name: _____

Predicting the Weather

How did you know what to wear today? Did you check the **weather forecast**? A weather forecast is a best guess, or estimate, of what the weather will be like.

Meteorologists are scientists who study the atmosphere to forecast the weather. They use weather instruments to gather information about what is going on in the atmosphere. They take measurements from the ground, the air, and outer space. They combine their observations with computer models and data on past weather patterns. Weather is hard to predict. The more data meteorologists collect, the more accurate their forecasts can be.

Weather Instruments

Thermometer: measures air temperature

Barometer: measures air pressure

Anemometer: measures wind speed

Rain gauge: collects and measures precipitation

Weather balloon: takes instruments high into the atmosphere

Satellite: photographs and tracks large air movements and storms

Doppler radar: detects amount of precipitation, wind direction, and speed

Weather forecasting is not exact. To help, meteorologists use probability based on past conditions. You may see a forecast that says that tomorrow there is a 60% chance of rain. This means that in the past, when atmospheric conditions were similar, it rained 60% of the time.

1. A *weather forecast* _____.
   a. observes and studies weather
   b. collects and measure precipitation
   c. predicts what the weather will be like

2. The more _____ *meteorologists* collect with their

   instruments, the more accurate their _____ will be.

3. If you see a weather forecast that predicts an 80% chance of snow, what does that mean?

   _____

   _____

Name: _____

Climate Patterns

Different parts of the world have different climates. **Climate** is the long-term pattern of weather in a place, measured over 30 years or more. Climate is usually defined by these factors:

➡ **Temperature:** both the average yearly temperature of a place and the difference between highest and lowest temperatures

➡ **Precipitation:** the amount of rain or snow an area gets in a year and in what part or parts of the year it falls

Climate Zones

Near the **equator**, the Sun rises high in the sky and shines for a long time each day. This means that climates close to the equator tend to be warm or hot. The North and South Poles are the farthest points away from the equator. They are always cold because the Sun shines on them at a low angle for a short time each day. Sometimes it doesn't shine at all. Earth can be divided into climate zones based on the amount of sunlight each area receives:

➡ **Tropical Zones:** Located along the equator, these zones receive strong sunlight all year long. They are hot and humid with a lot of rain.

➡ **Temperate Zones:** Climates in these zones usually have wide temperature ranges throughout the year as they experience four seasons.

➡ **Arctic Zones:** Farthest from the equator, these zones are cold all the time.

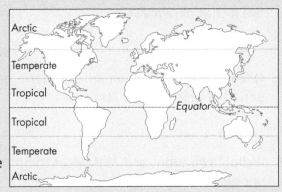

Distance to the equator is only one part of an area's climate. Other factors play a part as well:

Winds and Currents: The unequal heating of Earth causes air in the atmosphere and water in the oceans to flow and move. These **currents** move heat around Earth, warming some places more than others.

Geography: Places up high are cooler than places closer to sea level. Places closer to oceans have milder, wetter climates than places that are closer to the center of a continent.

1. *Climate* is _____.
   a. the weather patterns in a place over a long time
   b. how far from the equator a specific place is located
   c. air and water currents moving heat around Earth

2. An area's climate is usually defined by measuring _____

   and _____ over a long period of time.

3. Why do places near the equator tend to have warmer climates than places near the poles?

   _____

   _____

Name: _____

Weather or Climate Activity

Directions: Identify each example as either *weather* or *climate*.

1. The Amazon River Basin floods during the wet season.

   _____

2. The atmosphere has certain conditions at one place and time.

   _____

3. It rained heavily all last week, and the river came over its banks and flooded the town.

   _____

4. The Mojave Desert is very dry and gets an average of five inches of rain a year.

   _____

5. One place has specific weather patterns over a long period of time, at least 30 years.

   _____

6. It should be sunny and 75 degrees tomorrow for our picnic.

   _____

7. The rainy season in the Philippines starts in June and lasts until October.

   _____

8. The wind is currently blowing from the west at 10 miles an hour.

   _____

9. A blizzard warning is in effect for New York City. We are expecting winds greater than 35 miles per hour and heavy snow.

   _____

10. Mongolia has cold winters and short summers, with an average of 257 cloudless days a year.

    _____

Amazon village, Sascha Grabow (*www.saschagrabow.com*), CC BY-SA 3.0.

Name: _____

Humans Use Natural Resources

Think about all the things you use each day and where they came from. Where does paper come from? How are pencils made? What materials are your clothes made from? Everything you see is made from **natural resources**.

Natural resources are things found in nature that people can use, such as water, soil, air, sunlight, animals, trees, rocks, and oil. Everything we use, from pencils to video games to roller coasters, is made from natural resources. Pencils are made from wood, which comes from trees, and paper comes from trees as well. The dark, inner core of a pencil is made from graphite and clay, both **minerals** that come from Earth. Your clothes might be made of cotton from a plant or from **synthetic** fabrics made from oil.

Some natural resources are **renewable**. That means that we won't run out of them if we are careful. We will never run out of sunlight or wind. Fresh water and clean air are renewable, as long as we don't pollute them. Plants and animals are renewable resources because they reproduce, but we have to be careful not to use them faster than they can replace themselves.

Other resources are **nonrenewable**, which means that if we use them up, we cannot get more. **Fossil fuels** like oil, gas, coal, and minerals such as copper, iron, and aluminum take millions of years to form. They are nonrenewable because we use them faster than they can be replaced.

Renewable Resources

Resource	Source (where it comes from)	Ways We Can Use It
sunlight	the Sun	to keep warm; to grow food; for solar energy; to dry clothes
fresh water	the water cycle	drinking; bathing; cooking; cleaning
plants and trees	gathered from nature or grown in a garden or on a farm	for food; for clothing and other fabrics; to make medicines; wood; paper; rubber

Nonrenewable Resources

Resource	Source (where it comes from)	Ways We Can Use It
fossil fuels: oil, coal, natural gas	drilled or mined from Earth	burned to make electricity; burned to heat buildings; refined into gasoline for vehicles; used to make plastic
minerals and metal ore	mined from Earth	make metals, such as steel; used in electronics; buildings; glass; cans; foil

1. What is a *natural resource*? _____

2. Natural resources that we can't get more of once they are gone are called

   _____ resources.

3. Name three natural resources and how you use them.

   _____   _____

   _____   _____

   _____   _____

Name: _____

Word Study—Earth and Human Activity

Directions: Fill in the graphic organizer for the term *natural resources*.

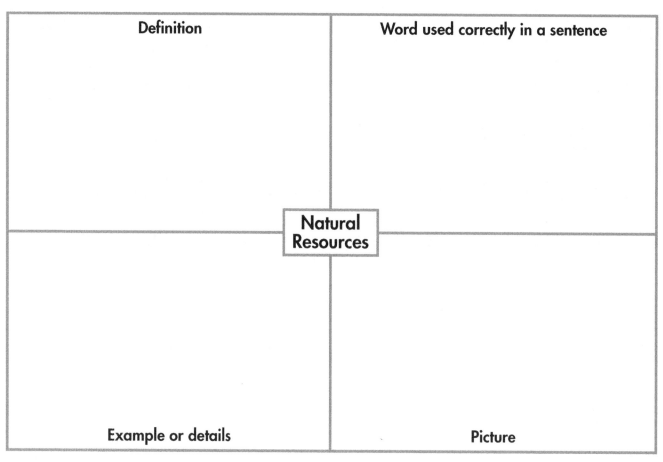

Definition	Word used correctly in a sentence
Example or details	**Picture**

Directions: Write a meaningful sentence to help you remember each vocabulary word.

1. **decompose**—to break down into the smallest possible parts; decay

   _____

2. **extract**—to remove or take out

   _____

3. **minerals**—a valuable or useful substance that is formed naturally in the ground

   _____

4. **nonrenewable**—a natural resource that, once used up, cannot be replaced

   _____

5. **renewable**—a natural resource that, if used carefully, will not run out

   _____

6. **synthetic**—made by humans; not natural

   _____

Name: _____

Using Natural Resources

There are more humans on Earth right now than there have ever been before. The world population is over seven billion and is growing every day. More people means we use more **natural resources**. It is important for everyone to have food to eat, clothes to wear, and shelter.

Where do we get all these resources? From Earth and the natural environment. We cut down trees, we dig fossil fuels and ore from the ground, and we pipe water into factories, businesses, schools, and homes. We cut down forests for farmland to grow food and to build houses.

We create problems when we **extract,** or take, resources from the environment. We also cause problems when we **transport** resources to where they are needed, and then **dispose** of them when we are done with them:

➡ When we extract natural resources from Earth, we often hurt the environment.

➡ When we cut down forests for farmland or mining, we lose the resources of the forests. We also take away the habitat of the animals and plants.

➡ When ships and trucks burn gasoline to carry food to where it is needed, we use up fossil fuels and create pollution.

➡ We use fossil fuels to make plastic packages for food. Once we've used the plastic packages, we throw them away. We fill landfills with plastic that does not **decompose**.

Humans need natural resources to live, but we are using more than we need. In some places the amount of resources used **per capita**, or per person, is getting larger all the time. What can we do? We can use fewer resources, and we can be careful about how we use the resources we really need. Instead of burning fossil fuels, we can generate electricity from solar and wind power. We can drive cleaner hybrid or electric cars, and we can take buses and trains and use bicycles whenever possible. We can eat food grown close to where we live, and buy items with less packaging. We can make less trash and recycle as much of our waste as possible. We can **conserve** fresh water by using only what we really need, and reduce water pollution by using nontoxic cleaners.

1. *Extract* means to _____.
   a. take or get   **b.** go or travel   **c.** grow or expand

2. There are problems with _____, or taking, natural resources,

_____ them to where they are needed, and

_____ of them when we are finished using them.

3. What is one way you could reduce the amount of natural resources you use?

_____

_____

Name: _____

The Problem with Plastic

How much plastic do you think you use and throw away? Think about all the different ways you use plastic:

- ➡ candy wrappers
- ➡ chip and cookie bags
- ➡ disposable cups and lids
- ➡ disposable spoons and forks
- ➡ food containers

- ➡ sandwich bags
- ➡ shopping bags
- ➡ straws
- ➡ toys
- ➡ water bottles and caps

Most of the plastic we use is **single-use plastic**, meaning we use it once and then we throw it away. It may seem like no big deal to throw away a straw or a chip bag, but you're not the only one doing it. Let's say you bring a sandwich for lunch in a plastic sandwich bag every day. After you eat your sandwich, you throw the bag in the trash. If there are 175 days in the school year, you throw away 175 bags a year. There are about 16 million students in the USA. If only half of the kids in the country throw away a plastic sandwich bag every day, that's 2.8 *billion* plastic sandwich bags being thrown away each year. And that's just sandwich bags. Imagine how much plastic we throw away altogether!

Plastic is made to last. It can take more than 500 years for a plastic sandwich bag to break down into small pieces. Even then, it never **decomposes** completely. If the first colonists kept their snacks in plastic bags 400 years ago, those plastic bags would still be around today!

Why do we use so much plastic? It's lightweight, cheap to make, and can be made into any shape. Some plastic products are important, such as medical instruments and car airbags. And plastics are used in things we use every day and don't throw away such as cell phones, televisions, and video game consoles. The problem is that most of the plastic produced today is single-use plastic, and we all use more than we need. Some plastic gets recycled, but a lot of single-use plastic is dropped as litter and ends up in the ocean where it harms sea life. Scientists think that if things continue as they are, by 2050, there will be more plastic than living organisms in Earth's oceans.

1. Which of the following is an example of a single-use plastic?
   a. napkin   **b.** straw   **c.** soda can

2. Plastic will not break down for hundreds of years and will never _____.

3. What single-use plastics have you used? _____

   What could you use instead? _____

Name: _____

Environmental Pros and Cons

Directions: For each action, list the **pros** and **cons** for both you and the environment. A *pro* is something that is good; a *con* is something that is not good. The first one has been done for you. For the third chart, choose your own action.

▶ **Action:** Ride a bike to school instead of riding in a car.

	Pros	Cons
Me	–saves gas –saves money –feel good about helping	–takes longer –have to pedal
The Environment	–saves gas –less pollution	

▶ **Action:** Use fewer single-use plastics.

	Pros	Cons
Me		
The Environment		

▶ **Action:** _____

	Pros	Cons
Me		
The Environment		

Name: _____

The Scientific Method

Scientists are people who answer questions by studying the world. They follow a process called the **scientific method**.

First, scientists need a **question to answer**. Usually, they make an observation about something that they don't understand, and then they ask a question about it.

Question: Why is my dog scratching so much?

Scientists do research to find out if anyone else has already answered the question. They look for information about the question they are studying. Then, scientists think of a possible answer to the question. It must be an idea that can be tested. They **predict** what will happen if their idea is correct. This is called a **hypothesis**.

Possible Answer: I think my dog might have fleas.

Hypothesis: If my dog has fleas, I will find some fleas on her.

Scientists **make observations** or **do experiments** to see if the results support their hypothesis.

Test: Look for fleas on my dog. Use a magnifying glass to look closely.

The test results may support the hypothesis or they may not. Depending on the results, scientists may ask new questions or revise their hypothesis. The scientific method is rarely a straight line from hypothesis to results.

If the results support the hypothesis...	If the results do not support the hypothesis...
The hypothesis is probably correct. *Result:* I found lots of fleas on my dog. Scientists then look for related questions that will help them understand the problem even better and test those questions. *New question:* Will a bath remove the fleas from my dog? *Test:* Give my dog a bath and check for fleas.	The hypothesis is probably not correct. It is time to revise the hypothesis, and do more tests. *Result:* I did not find any fleas on my dog. My dog probably isn't scratching because of fleas. *Revised hypothesis:* Maybe my dog has an allergy to grass. If my dog has an allergy to grass, her scratching will get worse when she plays on the grass at the park. *Test:* Take the dog to the park and watch for scratching.

Directions: Next to each statement, write the step of the scientific method.

Word Bank	hypothesis	question	research	result	test

1. Will bean plants grow taller when given orange juice? _____

2. Read about how plants grow and tests done on plants by other scientists. _____

3. If plants are given orange juice, they will grow taller than plants given plain water. _____

4. Give one bean plant water and give another bean plant orange juice. Measure the growth of the plants. _____

5. The plant given orange juice did not grow taller than the one given water. _____

6. In this experiment, the results **did**   **did not**   support the hypothesis. What question would you ask next?

_____

_____

Name: _____

Word Study—Science and Engineering

Directions: Write each vocabulary word in a meaningful sentence.

constraints—limitations that tell engineers what they can and cannot do

_____

_____

criteria—requirements of a project that tell engineers what they must create to solve the problem

_____

_____

experiment—a controlled test or investigation

_____

_____

hypothesis—testable prediction about what you expect to happen

_____

_____

Directions: List the steps for the scientific method and for the engineering design process.

The Scientific Method	The Engineering Design Process

Name: _____

What Do Scientists Study?

Natural scientists try to understand the natural world. Natural science can be divided into two main branches: life science and physical science.

Life Science
Biology, or **life science**, is the study of living things. These scientists study all kinds of life. Some study the smallest, single-celled animals. Others study the interactions of entire ecosystems. Fields of biology include the following:
- **Medicine:** the study, diagnosis, prevention, and treatment of human disease
- **Botany:** the study of plant life
- **Zoology:** the study of animal life

Dr. Jane Goodall

Dr. Jane Goodall is a world-famous zoologist. She studies the behavior of chimpanzees in Africa. She works with others to protect wild chimpanzees and their environment. She said, "My mission is to create a world where we can live in harmony with nature."

Physical Science
Physical science is the study of non-living things. Some scientists study energy, motion, and forces. Others study very small things that you can't see, such as atoms. Some fields in physical science are:
- **Physics:** the study of matter, energy, and the interactions between them
- **Chemistry:** study of substances and interactions
- **Earth Science:** the study of our planet
- **Astronomy:** the study of stars, planets, and space

Astronomer Wanda Diaz Merced studies stars by listening to them. Because she cannot see, she came up with a way to turn data from telescopes into sound. She finds patterns hidden in the information received from telescopes.

Some scientists study more than one branch of science at the same time. For instance, **biochemists** combine life science and physical science. They study the tiny parts that make up living things.

Directions: For each example, choose *life science* or *physical science*.

1. Rosalind Franklin studied DNA, the material that determines how a living thing will look and function.

   life science   **physical science**

2. Neil deGrasse Tyson observes stars and galaxies to try to understand how the universe was formed.

   life science   **physical science**

3. Ahmed Zwail won a Nobel Prize for studying how atoms in a molecule move during a chemical reaction.

   life science   **physical science**

4. Katherine Esau studied the effects of viruses on plants.

   life science   **physical science**

5. Charles Richter developed the scale that we use to measure the power of earthquakes.

   life science   **physical science**

6. Which types of science would you like to study? _____

   Why? _____

Name: _____

The Engineering Design Process

Engineers are people who solve problems using science, math, and technology. How do they solve these problems? They use a series of steps called the Engineering Design Process. First, engineers need to know the problem they want to solve. Then, they need to know two more important things: the **criteria** and the **constraints**.

Criteria are the requirements of a project. They tell engineers what they *must* create to solve the problem. When a project is completed, it will be successful if it meets all the criteria. For example:

- The roller coaster must meet all safety rules.
- The roller coaster must have two loops.

Constraints are limitations that tell the engineers what they *can* and *cannot* do. They tell what kinds of materials they can use, or how much space the solution can take up. Constraints might limit how long the project can take and usually limit the amount of money that can be spent. Engineers must also think about how a project might impact society and the environment. For example:

- The bridge must cost less than five million dollars.
- You can use only materials that will not rust.
- The project must be finished in one year.

Once engineers know the criteria and constraints of a project, they develop ideas for possible solutions. They research all aspects of the problem and how similar problems have been solved before. They brainstorm many ideas. Then, they narrow it down to several ideas they think might work. Many times, they find that they can combine the best parts of different solutions to create a new, better solution.

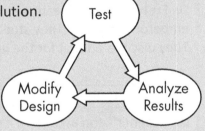

Once they have determined what they think is the best design, they test the design and analyze the results. They use the results to change or modify the design. Then, they test it again and repeat the cycle. Engineers may go through this cycle many times in order to reach the best possible result.

Directions: For each item, choose whether it is a *criteria* or a *constraint*. Remember this:

➡ If it tells what the finished project will do or look like, it is *criteria*.

➡ If it tells what the engineers can and can't do, it's a *constraint*.

1. The bridge must be high enough in the center for ships to pass under.   **criteria**   **constraint**

2. The project cannot take longer than six months.   **criteria**   **constraint**

3. You must use only waterproof materials.   **criteria**   **constraint**

4. The rocket must reach a speed of 7.9 kilometers per second.   **criteria**   **constraint**

5. The final product must be safe enough for a child to use.   **criteria**   **constraint**

Name: _____

Science or Engineering—What's the Difference?

Science

Scientists begin with a question, such as "Why do we dream?" or "What makes leaves change color in the fall?" They observe the natural world and do tests in order to *provide answers and explanations*. Scientists explore and investigate the world around us and show us what they find.

Engineering

Engineers begin with a problem, a need, or a desire, such as wanting to make an airplane fly higher or the need to use fewer fossil fuels. They design, test, and improve design ideas *to meet needs or solve problems*. Engineers provide creative solutions to real-world challenges in society.

Directions: Read each description and think about whether the person is a scientist or an engineer. Write which one you think he or she is, and why.

1 Eiji Nakatsu is a birdwatcher. He watches kingfishers dive into the water and come up with fish. He notices that the birds don't make a splash as they enter the water. He remembers that the fast-moving bullet trains he rides at home have a problem. They can't go fast through tunnels because the front of the train makes a booming noise in the air when it exits a tunnel. He thinks he can copy the shape of the kingfisher's beak on the nose of a bullet train to make it quieter.

_____

2 Dr. Fretwell and his team want to know if shrinking sea ice and rising temperatures are affecting emperor penguins. They studied satellite pictures of the penguin colony from the last 10 years. They discovered that for the last three years, none of the chicks have survived to become adults.

_____

3 Dr. Ozdener's son asked him if snakes smell with their tongues. This got him thinking about human tongues and how our sense of taste and smell seem connected. Dr. Ozdener and his team studied tongue cells. They found that the cells had both taste and smell receptors on them. This may help explain how smell and taste work together.

_____

4 When Dr. Mubenga was 17, she almost died. The hospital she was in didn't have enough gas for their generator. Dr. Mubenga always wanted to find a solution. Recently, she developed a way to make battery packs last longer and cost less. The battery packs can store solar energy to power generators even when the Sun isn't shining.

_____

Tracking Sheet

Unit 1 (pages 6–10)
Natural Resources	
Word Study—Natural and Synthetic	
Using Natural Resources	
Synthetic Materials—Plastic	
Natural vs. Synthetic	

Unit 2 (pages 11–15)
Physical and Chemical Changes	
Word Study—Physical and Chemical Change	
Evidence of Chemical Change	
Reversible and Irreversible Changes	
Which Kind of Change?	

Unit 3 (pages 16–20)
Non-Contact Forces	
Word Study—Non-Contact Forces	
Gravity	
Magnetic Force	
Attract or Repel?	

Unit 4 (pages 21–26)
What Is a Wave?	
Word Study—Mechanical Waves—Part 1	
Word Study—Mechanical Waves—Part 2	
Mechanical Waves	
Transverse Waves	
Longitudinal Waves	

Unit 5 (pages 27–30)
Electromagnetic Waves	
Word Study—Electromagnetic Waves	
Visible Light	
How We Use Electromagnetic Waves	

Unit 6 (pages 31–39)
Wave Amplitude—Part 1	
Wave Amplitude—Part 2	
Wavelength and Frequency	
Sound Waves and Light Waves	
Word Study—Measuring Waves	
Wave Behavior	
Mechanical and Electromagnetic Waves	
Wave Activity	

Unit 7 (pages 40–45)
Kinetic Energy and Potential Energy	
Word Study—Energy	
Energy Transformation	
Energy Transfer	
Energy Activities	
Energy Transformations	

Unit 8 (pages 46–50)
Cells	
Word Study—Human Cells	
Cell Structure and Function	
Animal Cell	
Cell Division in Your Body	

Unit 9 (pages 51–55)
Human Body Systems	
Your Respiratory System	
Your Nervous System	
Word Study—Human Body Systems	
Review and Write—Human Body Systems	

Unit 10 (pages 56–60)
How Your Senses Work	
Word Study—Senses	
Your Senses at Work	
More Than Five Senses	
Animal Senses	

Unit 11 (pages 61–65)
Your Genes and Your Environment	
Genotype and Phenotype	
Word Study—Heredity	
Inherited and Acquired Traits	
Healthy Human Habits	

Unit 12 (pages 66–70)
Reproduction	
Word Study—Reproduction	
Animal Courtship and Competition	
Flowering-Plant Reproduction	
Which Kind of Reproduction?	

Unit 13 (pages 71–75)
Ecosystems	
Word Study—Ecosystems	
Patterns of Interaction	
Ecosystem Interactions	
Change in Ecosystems	

Unit 14 (pages 76–80)
Gravity and Our Solar System	
Word Study—Our Solar System	
Moon Movement	
Is Pluto a Planet?	
Telescopes	

Unit 15 (pages 81–86)
The Hydrologic Cycle	
Word Study—Earth Cycles	
The Rock Cycle—Heat and Pressure	
The Rock Cycle—Weathering and Erosion	
Follow the Rock Activity	
Energy Flow and Earth Cycles	

Unit 16 (pages 87–91)
Inside Earth	
Word Study—Plate Tectonics	
Tectonic Plate Boundaries	
The Biggest Changes on Earth	
Plate Tectonics Activity	

Unit 17 (pages 92–96)
Weather or Climate?	
Word Study—Weather and Climate	
Predicting the Weather	
Climate Patterns	
Weather or Climate Activity	

Unit 18 (pages 97–101)
Humans Use Natural Resources	
Word Study—Earth and Human Activity	
Using Natural Resources	
The Problem with Plastic	
Environmental Pros and Cons	

Unit 19 (pages 102–106)
The Scientific Method	
Word Study—Science and Engineering	
What Do Scientists Study?	
The Engineering Design Process	
Science or Engineering—What's the Difference?	

Answer Key

Unit 1—Natural and Synthetic

Natural Resources (page 6)

1. c
2. Check for appropriate answers.
3. Check for appropriate answers.

Word Study—Natural and Synthetic Materials (page 7)

Check for appropriate sentences.

Using Natural Resources (page 8)

1. False
2. d
3. Check for appropriate answers.

Synthetic Materials—Plastic (page 9)

1. a
2. Check for appropriate answers.
3. Check for appropriate answers.

Natural vs. Synthetic (page 10)

1.

	Natural Grass	Synthetic Grass
Advantages	Soft and cool Doesn't hurt when you fall on it It is a renewable resource	Will last a long time Harder to rip up Doesn't need to be watered or mowed
Disadvantages	Needs water Needs fertilizer Needs mowing and weeding	Expensive Can hurt when you slide or fall on it, and it gets hot. Made from nonrenewable resources

2. Check for appropriate answers.

Unit 2—Physical and Chemical Changes

Physical and Chemical Changes (page 11)

1. b
2. substance
3. A chemical change always produces a new substance, but a physical change does not.

Word Study—Physical and Chemical Change (page 12)

Check for appropriate examples of each term.

1. matter
2. substance
3. properties
4. state of matter
5. molecule
6. physical change
7. chemical change
8. irreversible
9. evidence

Evidence of Chemical Change (page 13)

1. a
2. Nothing
3. You can tell a chemical change has happened if there is a change in color or smell, formation of gas, or emission of heat or light.

Reversible and Irreversible Changes (page 14)

1. physical, reversible
2. physical, irreversible
3. physical, reversible
4. chemical, irreversible
5. physical, reversible
6. physical, irreversible
7. chemical, irreversible

Which Kind of Change? (page 15)

Check for appropriate explanations.

1. physical, irreversible
2. chemical, irreversible
3. physical, reversible
4. chemical, irreversible
5. Check for appropriate drawings and explanations.

Unit 3—Non-Contact Forces

Non-Contact Forces (page 16)

1. d
2. Gravitational
3. Electromagnetic
4. Contact forces have to touch things to act on them. Non-contact forces do not have to touch things to act on them.

Word Study—Non-Contact Forces (page 17)

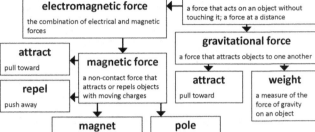

Gravity (page 18)

1. a
2. mass
3. Check for appropriate answers.
4. marble 1, human 2, elephant 3, mountain 4, Moon 5, Earth 6, Sun 7

Magnetic Force (page 19)

1. c
2. south, north
3. poles
4.

Attract or Repel? (page 20)

1. They will repel each other because the magnetic lines of force are moving in opposite directions.
2. The magnets will pull toward each other (attract) because the magnetic lines of force are moving in the same direction.
3. ferromagnetic

Unit 4—Mechanical Waves

What Is a Wave? (page 21)

1. b
2. medium
3. A wave is a way that energy moves from place to place.

Word Study—Mechanical Waves—Part 1 (page 22)

Check for appropriate sentences.

1. particles
2. medium
3. mechanical waves
4. waves
5. matter

Word Study—Mechanical Waves—Part 2 (page 23)

Check for appropriate drawings.

1. longitudinal wave
2. transverse wave
3. Perpendicular
4. Parallel
5. longitudinal

Check for explanations.

Mechanical Waves (page 24)

1. a
2. matter or a medium
3. solid, liquid, gas

Transverse Waves (page 25)

1. perpendicular
2. The wave would move along the rope and the rope itself would move side to side.
3. Transverse—It would be a transverse wave because the rope is moving perpendicular to the wave.

Longitudinal Waves (page 26)

1. parallel
2. The wave would move along the Slinky and the Slinky itself would move up and down.
3. Transverse—The Slinky is moving perpendicular to the wave.

Answer Key *(cont.)*

Unit 5—Electromagnetic Waves

Electromagnetic Waves (page 27)

1. a
2. matter, empty space
3. visible light waves

Word Study—Electromagnetic Waves (page 28)

Check for appropriate answers.

Visible Light (page 29)

1. c
2. red, violet
3. *Example answer:* When light hits an object, some wavelengths of light are reflected and some are absorbed. We see the light that is reflected. When we look at green grass, we see the green wavelengths of light that are reflected.

How We Use Electromagnetic Waves (page 30)

1. a
2. visible
3. Check for appropriate answers. *Examples:* We use visible light waves from a light bulb to see in the dark; we use X-rays to see people's bones.

Unit 6—Measuring Waves

Wave Amplitude—Part 2 (page 32)

1.
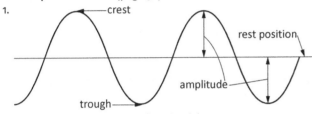

2. b
3. crests; energy (amplitude)
4. energy

Wavelength and Frequency (page 33)

1. b
2. a
3. Check for appropriate labels and drawings. They should be similar to the high-frequency and low-frequency examples.
4. b; This higher-frequency wave has more energy than the lower-frequency wave.

Sound Waves and Light Waves (page 34)

1. b
2. Thunder sound waves have a long wavelength and a low frequency.
3. radio waves
4. Volume
   Pitch
5. The wavelength and wave frequency of a light wave tell us what kind of wave it is.

Word Study—Measuring Waves (page 35)

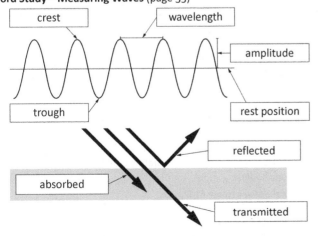

Wave Behavior (page 37)

1. absorbed
2. reflected
3. reflected
4. transmitted
5. absorbed
6. transmitted

Mechanical and Electromagnetic Waves (page 38)

Guide students to see that the two kinds of waves have more similarities than differences.

	Ocean Wave	Sound Wave	Visible Light Wave
Is it electromagnetic or mechanical?	mechanical	mechanical	electromagnetic
Is it transverse or longitudinal?	transverse	longitudinal	transverse
Does it require a medium?	yes	yes	no
Does it transport energy?	yes	yes	yes
Does it transport matter?	no	no	no
Does it absorb, reflect, and transmit?	yes	yes	yes
Does it have a wavelength and frequency?	yes	yes	yes
Does it have an amplitude?	yes	yes	yes

Wave Activity (page 39)

1. d
2. d
3. b
4. b
5. a

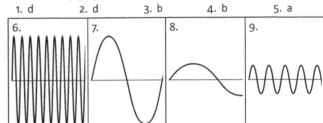

Unit 7—Energy

Kinetic Energy and Potential Energy (page 40)

1. kinetic, potential
2. stored (or saved)
3. moving
4. kinetic
   potential
   kinetic
   kinetic
   potential

Word Study—Energy (page 41)

1. energy transfer
2. thermal energy
3. kinetic energy
4. mechanical energy
5. potential energy
6. speed
7. mass
8. gravitational
9. energy transformation

Energy Transformation (page 42)

1. b
2. created, destroyed
3. light, heat, sound (from trapped gasses expanding)

Energy Transfer (page 43)

1. c
2. more
3. faster
4. The car traveling fast is more dangerous because it has more kinetic energy and will cause more damage if it hits something.

Answer Key *(cont.)*

Energy Activities (page 44)

1. potential, kinetic
2. kinetic, potential
3. kinetic, potential
4. potential, kinetic

5–10. Check for appropriate drawings and labels.

Example answers:

5. anything moving
6. anything putting out heat
7. anything putting out light
8. anything putting out sound
9. plants, food, battery
10. anything above Earth's surface

Energy Transformations (page 45)

1. chemical, electrical
2. electrical, thermal (heat)
3. electrical, light
4. mechanical, sound
5. light, chemical

Unit 8—Human Cells

Cells (page 46)

1. c
2. living organisms (or living things)
3. Because living cells can only come from the same kind of living cells; mushrooms can only come from mushroom cells.

Word Study—Human Cells (page 47)

Check for appropriate sentences.

Cell Structure and Function (page 48)

1. b
2. function or job
3. To hold the cell together and to control what moves into and out of the cell

Animal Cell (page 49)

1. *cell membrane:* surrounds the cell and holds it together, controls what moves into and out of the cell
2. *nucleus:* directs all the cell's activities, contains the DNA that is the information for making more cells
3. *cytoplasm:* gives the cell its shape, has chemicals in it called enzymes that break down food and other substances so the cell can use them
4. *organelles:* work together to keep the cell alive

Cell Division in Your Body (page 50)

1. a
2. growth, maintenance, repair—Check examples.
3. Neurons can't divide to repair injury, so we need to take care of the ones we have.

Unit 9—Human Body Systems

Human Body Systems (page 51)

1. a
2. systems
3. The body dies because the systems rely on one another, and if one stopped working, the others couldn't do their jobs.

Your Respiratory System (page 52)

1. a
2. oxygen
3. The epiglottis covers your trachea (airway) when you swallow so no food or liquid goes into your lungs.

Your Nervous System (page 53)

1. b
2. Neurons or Nerve cells
3. If we had to think about them all the time, we couldn't do much else, and we might forget and die!

Word Study—Human Body Systems (page 54)

1. cells
2. tissue
3. organ
4. organ system
5. nervous system
6. respiratory system
7. circulatory system

Review and Write—Human Body Systems (page 55)

1.

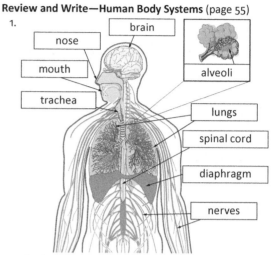

2. diaphragm
3. mouth, nose
4. trachea, lungs
5. alveoli, blood
6. Check for appropriate answers.

Unit 10—Senses

How Your Senses Work (page 56)

1. b
2. nerve signals, nerves, brain
3. create memories; respond with a thought, decision, or physical action

Word Study—Senses (page 57)

1. senses
2. sensory organ
3. sensory receptors
4. stimuli
5. brain
6. neurons
7. memories
8. response

Check for appropriate examples.

Your Senses at Work (page 58)

Sense	Sensory Organ	Type of Stimuli Detected
sight	eyes	*Electromagnetic (light)*
hearing	ears	mechanical (sound waves)
touch	*skin*	mechanical (pressure)
taste	tongue	*chemical*
smell	*nose*	chemical

Stimulus	Sensory Organ	Possible Response
a very bright light	*Eyes*	*Close eyes*
a bad smell	*Nose*	*Pinch your nose, make a face, move away*
a sip of spoiled milk	*Tongue*	*Spit it out*
your friend whispering to you very quietly	*Ears*	*Say, "What?"; lean closer, cup hand to ear*
brushing up against a cactus	*Skin*	*Say, "Ouch"; jump away, brush off spines*

More Than Five Senses (page 59)

1. c
2. inner ear, eyes
3. *Proprioception* is your sense of your own body. It is important because it allows us to accurately control the movement of our bodies.

Animal Senses (page 60)

1. a
2. ultraviolet and infrared
3. Check for appropriate answers.

Answer Key (cont.)

Unit 11—Heredity

Your Genes and Your Environment (page 61)
1. b
2. genes and environment
3. Check for appropriate answers.

Genotype and Phenotype (page 62)
1. c
2. genotype, environment
3. Flamingos are pink because they eat pink shrimp and algae.
4. phenotype

Word Study—Heredity (page 63)
1. controls a cell's growth; passes information from parent to offspring
2. Check for appropriate answers.
3. Check for appropriate answers, such as amount of sun or cold weather
4. An inherited trait passes from parent to offspring, while an acquired trait is from the environment and not from genes.
5. A genotype is an organism's gene information, while a phenotype is the observable characteristics of an organism.

Inherited and Acquired Traits (page 64)
1. c   3. b   5. a   7. b
2. a   4. c   6. b   8. b

Healthy Human Habits (page 65)
1. False
2. Check for appropriate answers.
3. Check for appropriate answers.

Unit 12—Reproduction

Reproduction (page 66)
1. c
2. asexual, genetic
3. Asexual reproduction can be done by one organism and sexual reproduction requires cells from two different organisms.

Word Study—Reproduction (page 67)
Check for appropriate sentences.

Animal Courtship and Competition (page 68)
1. a
2. genes, offspring
3. large or colorful traits, song or dance, build nests or structures

Flowering-Plant Reproduction (page 69)
1. b
2. possible answers: water, wind, by bursting seed pods, carried by humans and animals
3. If they are under the parent plant, they won't have as much space to grow, and the parent plant can block the sunlight they need.

Which Kind of Reproduction? (page 70)
1. sexual   3. asexual   5. asexual   7. asexual
2. asexual   4. sexual   6. sexual

Unit 13—Ecosystems

Ecosystems (page 71)
1. a
2. compete, resources
3. The rabbit population would grow. They might eat all the grass.

Word Study—Ecosystems (page 72)
1. competition   4. organism   7. drivers
2. biotic factors   5. resources
3. interdependence   6. abiotic factors

Patterns of Interaction (page 73)
1. Competition   2. c   3. blood (food)

Ecosystem Interactions (page 74)
1. competition   4. competition
2. predation   5. predation
3. symbiosis

Change in Ecosystems (page 75)
1. c
2. driver, process
3. Answer should include an explanation of one of these: natural disaster, invasive species, pollution, resource use

Unit 14—Our Solar System

Gravity and Our Solar System (page 76)
1. a
2. mass
3. The Sun's gravity is strong enough because it has so much mass compared to the planets.

Word Study—Our Solar System (page 77)
1. planet   4. gravity   7. solar eclipse
2. astronomer   5. orbit   8. lunar cycle
3. mass   6. lunar eclipse

Moon Movement (page 78)
1. a   3. Moon, Earth
2. phases, lunar cycle   4. Earth, Moon

Is Pluto a Planet? (page 79)
1. Yes, Evidence: "Pluto's orbit around the Sun is oval shaped"
2. Yes, Evidence: "Pluto is round"
3. No, Evidence: "Pluto shares its orbital neighborhood with lots of other objects"

Telescopes (page 80)
1. c
2. Space, orbit
3. Stars begin to twinkle because their light is bent by Earth's atmosphere.

Unit 15—Earth Cycles

The Hydrologic Cycle (page 81)
1. b   2. c   3. in the oceans
4. The ice may have been there so long because it hasn't melted. It stays cold in Antarctica.

Word Study—Earth Cycles (page 82)
Part One
1. evaporates   2. condenses   3. precipitation
Part Two
4. weather   5. sediment   6. erosion   7. deposited
Part Three
igneous—a   metamorphic—b   sedimentary—c
lava—e   magma—d

The Rock Cycle—Heat and Pressure (page 83)
1. c
2. metamorphic
3. It is formed when magma or lava cools and hardens.

The Rock Cycle—Weathering and Erosion (page 84)
1. c
2. Weathering breaks rocks, and erosion moves the pieces.
3. Deposited sediments layer over one another and are pressed together.

Follow the Rock Activity (page 85)
1. Igneous rock gets turned into sediment by weathering and carried downhill by erosion. The sediment settles on the bottom of the ocean and is covered by more and more layers of sediment. The pressure creates sedimentary rock.
2. Sedimentary rock is forced underground. It is heated and squeezed until it changes into metamorphic rock.
3. Metamorphic rock is forced to the surface. Then, it gets turned into sediment by weathering and carried downhill by erosion. The sediment settles on the bottom of the ocean and is covered by more and more layers of sediment. The pressure creates sedimentary rock.

Answer Key *(cont.)*

Energy Flow and Earth Cycles (page 86)
1. heat from the Sun and heat from inside Earth
2. air, water
3. In both water and rock cycles, matter changes states through heating and cooling.

Unit 16—Plate Tectonics
Inside Earth (page 87)
1. c
2. crust
3. Check for appropriate answers.

Word Study—Plate Tectonics (page 88)
1. continents
2. tectonic plates
3. boundary
4. supercontinent
5. evidence
6. fossil

Check for appropriate drawings, examples, or sentences.

Tectonic Plate Boundaries (page 89)
1. c
2. a. convergent b. transform c. divergent
3. Magma oozes or erupts from the opening between the plates and hardens into solid rock.

The Biggest Changes on Earth (page 90)
1. a
2. tectonic plates
3. A supercontinent where all the current continents were joined together.

Plate Tectonics Activity (page 91)
1.
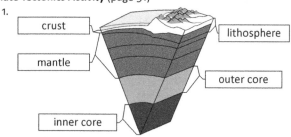

crust | mantle | lithosphere | outer core | inner core

2. *Convergent boundary*: Two plates push into each other; mountains and volcanoes form; earthquakes may occur
3. *Divergent boundary*: Plates move away from each other; magma comes up through the opening and forms new crust
4. *Transform boundary*: Two plates slide past each other; earthquakes may occur

Unit 17—Weather and Climate
Weather or Climate? (page 92)
1. b
2. pattern, a long period of time
3. *Weather* tells what is going on with the atmosphere for a short time, and *climate* is a pattern of weather over a long period of time.

Word Study—Weather and Climate (page 93)
Weather—at one time, day-to-day
Climate—pattern, long time
Both—temperature, precipitation, atmosphere
Check for appropriate sentences. More than one word can be used in a sentence.

Predicting the Weather (page 94)
1. c
2. data, forecasts
3. In the past, when the atmosphere was about the same, it snowed 80% of the time.

Climate Patterns (page 95)
1. a
2. temperature, precipitation
3. Near the equator, the Sun rises high in the sky and shines for a long time each day. The poles are colder because the Sun shines on them at a low angle and sometimes doesn't shine at all.

Weather or Climate Activity (page 96)
1. climate
2. weather
3. weather
4. climate
5. climate
6. weather
7. climate
8. weather
9. weather
10. climate

Unit 18—Earth and Human Activity
Humans Use Natural Resources (page 97)
1. something found in nature that people can use
2. nonrenewable
3. Check for appropriate sentences.

Word Study—Earth and Human Activity (page 98)
Check for appropriate organizers and sentences.

Using Natural Resources (page 99)
1. a
2. extracting, transporting, disposing
3. Check for appropriate answers.

The Problem with Plastic (page 100)
1. b
2. decompose
3. Check for appropriate answers.

Environmental Pros and Cons (page 101)
Check for appropriate answers.

Unit 19—Science and Engineering
The Scientific Method (page 102)
1. question
2. research
3. hypothesis
4. test
5. result
6. did not;
   Check for appropriate answers.

Word Study—Science and Engineering (page 103)
Possible answers:

▪ **Scientists** begin with a question to answer ▪ Predict and form a hypothesis ▪ Make observations or do experiments ▪ Explore and analyze ▪ Provide explanations	▪ **Engineers** begin with a problem ▪ Meet needs ▪ Solve problems ▪ Provide solutions to real world challenges

Check for appropriate answers.

What Do Scientists Study? (page 104)
1. life science
2. physical science
3. physical science
4. life science
5. physical science
6. Check for appropriate answers.

The Engineering Design Process (page 105)
1. criteria
2. constraint
3. constraint
4. criteria
5. criteria

Science or Engineering—What's the Difference? (page 106)
1. Mr. Nakatsu is an engineer because he is solving the train problem.
2. Dr. Fretwell is a scientist because he is trying to answer a question about penguins.
3. Dr. Ozdener is a scientist because he is trying to answer a question about tongue cells.
4. Dr. Mubenga is an engineer because she is trying to solve a problem about energy.

Made in the USA
Las Vegas, NV
23 December 2021

39293208R00063